Community Building

The Community College as Catalyst

Paul A. Elsner
Janet Beauchamp Clift

Community College Press®
a division of the American Association of Community Colleges

Washington, D.C.

The American Association of Community Colleges (AACC) is the primary advocacy organization for the nation's community colleges. The association represents 1,100 two-year, associate degree–granting institutions and more than 10 million students. AACC promotes community colleges through six strategic action areas: national and international recognition and advocacy for community colleges, learning and accountability, leadership development, economic and workforce development, connectedness across AACC membership, and international and intercultural education. Information about AACC and community colleges may be found at www.aacc.nche.edu.

Community College Press
American Association of Community Colleges
One Dupont Circle, NW
Suite 410
Washington, DC 20036

Printed in the United States of America.

ISBN 0-87117-336-0

*Our challenge is not to create a desired future but to
understand the future that is already developing around us.
From many points of view, our challenge is to get out of the
way of the positive movements which exist around us. We need
to connect people and organizations that are aware of the new
dynamics of our time. We need to substitute organic images
and processes for the mechanical ones with which
we have lived for so long.*
(1994)
—Robert Theobald, 1927–1999

This book is dedicated to the memory of Robert "Bob" Theobald, author, futurist, and global community builder in his own special way. We believe he was always right and ahead of his time.

Theobald managed to integrate the many facets of change from his 30-plus years of consulting work in communities, corporations, nonprofit organizations, state agencies, legislative bodies, educational institutions, religious groups, and presidential commissions. His main premise was that significant numbers of social entrepreneurs have moved beyond the broad spectrum of unreasoned optimism and stifling despair to realistic hope. Theobald believed that healthy human beings want to grow and help others to grow.

Trained as an economist, Theobald was also described as a futurist and was invited to speak in all of the 50 states and in many other countries. He contrasted social entrepreneurship and spiritual motivations to community building in his book *The Rapids of Change,* and he studied the enabling aspects of community development in *The Rich and the Poor, The Challenge of Abundance, Free Men and Free Markets, An Alternative Future for America, Futures Conditional, Economizing Abundance,* and *Habit and Habitat.*

Contents

Illustrations

Foreword

Community colleges proudly carry the word *community* in their title and lay claim to "building" their communities as an important part of their mission. The varying methodologies used by institutions in accomplishing this priority, however, are not well developed or well understood. Part of the reason might be the financial incentive system, which is heavily based on buying student seat time, as well as a lack of attention from practitioners and community college leaders to the underlying assumptions and theories behind community building.

As a large community college district, Maricopa comes close to having a districtwide vision of "building community." Ably led by Chancellor Paul Elsner for more than 20 years and blessed with a supportive governing board for much of that time, the district created a support structure and instituted several programs that formed the core of its methodology. How the district has learned from these programs to move its vision forward is the subject of this book.

Not every community college will be able to implement all the programs presented in this book, nor should they. All community colleges and their leaders can benefit by being more informed about the thinking and planning that led to the adoption of such programs. It is important, therefore, that exemplary programs in community colleges be documented so they can be shared with other colleges and passed along to future leaders. Although change will eventually bring with it a factor of obsolescence, the thinking, planning, and strategizing that went into these programs is timeless and will continue to inform and educate community college leaders for many years to come.

David R. Pierce
President Emeritus, American Association of Community Colleges

Preface

Human beings need community. As the poet W. H. Auden said, "We make friends or die." A survivor of the Oklahoma City bombing said it this way: "Where people feel no sense of belonging to a community, they are more likely to destroy it."

Community colleges adopted that term as their essential descriptor during their era of greatest expansion, the 1960s and 1970s. Although community colleges generally emphasize the core functions of teaching, college transfer, and the basic business of education over service to the community, these traditional functions, as well as the partnerships with business that are usually described as workforce development, do involve valuable community connections. Not only are they vitally important to the college mission, these functions build a more resilient, interdependent community.

In 1980, Edmund J. Gleazer Jr., president of the American Association of Community and Junior Colleges (now the American Association of Community Colleges [AACC]), wrote *Values, Vision, and Vitality*, a philosophical blueprint for community colleges to follow as they made the transition from traditional junior colleges to community builders and catalysts.

In 1988, the Commission on the Future of Community Colleges put community building at the center of a new vision in *Building Communities: A Vision for a New Century:*

> We propose . . . that the theme "Building Communities"
> become the new rallying point for the community college
> in America. We define the term "community" not only as a
> region to be served, but also as a climate to be created. (7)

The commission suggested that *community* includes activities in the classroom; in the college as a whole; and in relation to local, national, and international communities.

In *The Community-Building College: Leading the Way to Community Revitalization* (AACC 1996), Ervin L. Harlacher and James F. Gollattscheck reinforced the idea of incorporating community into the institution's philosophical framework. The *Building Communities* report (Commission 1988, 7) quotes John W. Gardner's 1987 Harry S. Truman Lecture to the AACC, in which he proposed that community colleges can become effective conveners:

> The college can perform a convening function at which representatives of various fragments and interests come together in unofficial but serious discussions of community problems.

But how committed is the average community college to community building? What do the colleges see as their community-building roles? Is there agreement on these roles among faculty leaders, boards of trustees, policymakers, and chief executive officers (CEO)? This book highlights our community-building experiences at Arizona's Maricopa Community College District (MCCD), which we believe might serve as models for others.

In the introduction we describe MCCD's structure and scope. Chapter 1 provides an overview of key elements of community building and reveals some of our experiences, which we hope will give readers some insight into community development from a practitioner's point of view. We believe community colleges can advance beyond episodic programs to a more engaged level of collaboration with their communities.

Community colleges' commitment to community building is complicated by national and state policy. Chapter 2 reviews some of the authorities, mandates, and covenants that affect community building.

What is the legal mandate for community development? How can a community college create a mandate when the governing charters and statutes are not clear? We hope this book will aid in constructive discussion and exploration of these issues. Chapter 2 also addresses the pressures community colleges face to balance a social agenda with a free-market agenda, which often compete for the same resources. We used MCCD as an example of how colleges must serve these two masters.

Chapters 3 and 4 include observations about our work with communities, which took place in local, targeted neighborhoods and through regional coalitions. We call the former *micro-community development*; the latter, *macro-community development*. Chapter 3 focuses on neighborhood development in Phoenix's Garcia Neighborhood Project. The collaboration among schools, community colleges, and private industry provides a model for urban renewal. Chapter 4 concentrates on the Phoenix Think Tank and the East Valley Think Tank, two working models of community coalitions undertaken with K–16 and community collaboration. We also look at several activities that resulted from these collaborations, such as neighborhood renewal efforts and the creation, together with community-based organizations, of Family Resource Centers.

Community building is a complex task, particularly in multicollege systems. Chapter 5 outlines lessons we have learned and makes some recommendations to those who undertake the task. Chapter 6 concludes the book with observations by several people experienced with and committed to community building.

Not all community colleges support community building. Appendixes A and B show the results of two surveys of community college presidents and chancellors. The Appendix A survey, conducted in March 2000 as part of the research for this book, was designed to indicate how some of the largest urban community college systems have addressed college personnel's direct engagement in communities. Respondents consisted of members of the RC-2000 federation (*renewal* and *change*). Twenty-two of the 25 CEOs who represent colleges dedicated to renewal and change indicated that few policies or procedures exist to mandate or procedurally support community volunteerism among faculty and staff.

The Appendix B survey was administered to 55 college CEOs at the AACC Presidents Academy Summer Institute in Breckenridge, Colorado, in July 2000. Respondents indicated on a scale from 0 to 11 the level of support for community building among each of four categories: board members, presidents, staff, and faculty. Although there was not a wide range of discrepancy, results indicated that college CEOs took the lead in community efforts. Appendixes C and D are samples of topics and exercises used during community-building workshops.

Unless otherwise noted, direct quotations are from interviews the authors conducted for this book.

We wish to acknowledge the many people in the nation's community colleges who help strengthen their communities through the difficult process of community building. We appreciate the Maricopa Community College District's dedication to its community and the community-building focus, energy, and creativity of its personnel.

Community colleges, we believe, should not look at themselves as being separate from the community. The community is part of the college and the college is part of the community. We wrote this book to enhance understanding about community colleges' powerful efficacy as community builders beyond academic services. Our wish is that more community colleges will engage in community building, not only because of its huge educational potential but also because it is their civic responsibility.

Paul A. Elsner
Janet Beauchamp Clift
Maricopa Community College District

Introduction: The Maricopa Community College District

Nine of the 14 counties in the state of Arizona have organized community college districts. The Maricopa County Community College District—its official name—is referred to as the Maricopa Community Colleges (MCC) or MCCD. It is one of the largest community college districts in the nation, serving more than 240,000 persons annually within the 9,226-square-mile county. MCCD consists of 10 separately accredited colleges, two skills centers, and several education centers and branches.

MCCD maintains a robust university-transfer program. Arizona State University (ASU), a large, comprehensive research university in Tempe, receives more than 65 percent of its upper-division transfers from the colleges, and 80 percent of the University of Phoenix's graduates have completed a major portion of their lower-division course work at MCCD. Assessment data indicate that MCCD students do as well as or better than those who did their freshman year in a university, once they reach the upper divisions of four-year institutions (Day 1999).

MCCD also has a strong record in industrial and corporate training, the result of a concerted effort to promote the economic development of the region. At any given time, 50 to 60 industries have contractual training arrangements with the colleges. These industries account for a major share of Arizona's job-creation rate—85,000 to 100,000 new jobs a year (Jarman 1999). The colleges' training capacity is the central attraction for many industries that relocate to Maricopa County, and it has become part of the economic portfolio for Arizona. While Phoenix's competition for new business once included only such U.S. cities as Austin, Texas; Sacramento, California; and Salt Lake City, Utah, it now includes Singapore, suburban Brussels, Ireland, and hundreds of other business environments around the world. Along with other influential factors—a favorable taxation policy, an unfettered regulatory environment, and a high quality of life—MCCD's training capacity attracts new businesses to the county.

More than 60 high-tech companies have contracted with MCCD, which in 1998 provided more than 85,000 person-hours of training—equivalent to the enrollment of Phoenix College or Scottsdale Community College—to Motorola alone. In addition to high tech, the district serves more than 400 occupational or career clusters, and more than 4,000 courses are activated each year from MCCD course banks.

Examples of MCCD special initiatives and projects include the following:

- Rio Salado College, a nontraditional distance-education college, offers hundreds of online courses and has enjoyed robust annual enrollment growth over the last five years.

- Mesa College trains a national cadre of community college leaders. Its Division Chair Academy assists department chairs and academic leaders with such issues as technology transformation, conflict resolution, and multicultural programs.

- MCCD led the development of the National Institute for Leadership Development (NILD). Funded by the Ford Foundation, NILD has trained close to 4,000 women for promotion to all levels of community college management and leadership. Carrole Wolin, NILD's executive director, reports that 80 percent of women currently in CEO positions in higher education around the country are products of the institute.

- MCCD was an early charter member of Campus Compact, a consortium that promotes service learning in universities and colleges. Students are connected with hundreds of community-based organizations to gain volunteer and service-learning experiences. In this way, MCCD carries out important social agendas that affect the quality of life in the region. One student described the campus philosophy as "whatever it takes" to connect college to community.

- MCCD supports an alternative high school within Chandler-Gilbert Community College, a charter high school at GateWay Community College, and dual-enrollment programs at all colleges. More than 5,000 students a year take community college and high school courses in both dual enrollment and concurrent enrollment courses, improving the high school graduation rate from 20 percent to 50 percent among participating students.

- Each of the MCCD colleges supports teacher recruitment and preparation through local school support programs or by direct preservice courses on the campuses. In addition, the district office has created a Teacher Education Committee to provide cross support among education faculty, has created a Teacher Education Partnership Commission with more than 40 community and education leaders, and has instigated the development of National Association for Community College Teacher Education programs. Recognizing the national crisis of the shortage in quality teachers, MCCD's chancellor and board have made teacher education a major focus, and it has been added to the board goals.

- MCCD is working with one of its community partners, an inner-city school district, to create a charter high school focusing on math and science.

- In 1990, MCCD instigated the development of RC-2000, a federation of large urban community college districts that promotes renewal and change (RC). The purpose of the group is to exchange best practices among top-level college administrators and national association executives. Through dialogues, publications, and site visits, they work to enhance the image of community colleges in policy and learning environments. The organization's 26 member institutions include the largest community colleges in the United States, the United Kingdom, and Canada. MCCD staff coordinate the group's activities and meetings. RC-2000 CEOs meet twice a year, each time in a different member city, focusing on a topic with urban impact. The federation also produces *The Urban Report,* a publication of colleges' best practices and the challenges facing urban college leaders.

All of these MCCD projects go beyond outreach to create the kind of networks that are the foundation of community building.

Chapter 1

What Is Community Building?

> *No society can remain vital or even survive without a reasonable base of shared values. . . .Where community exists it confers upon its members identity, a sense of belonging, a measure of security. Individuals acquire a sense of self partly from their continuous relations to others, and from the culture of their native place.*
>
> **—John W. Gardner (1991)**

Community building involves creating relationships that let people and organizations share values, find common interests, and mobilize resources toward solutions. For community colleges, this community building means reaching beyond the walls of their institutions to nurture such relationships and develop networks. Uniquely positioned to be neutral conveners, community colleges can bring parties together and bind divergent interests for the betterment of the community.

Community building is more than making a whole from the sum of its parts. It involves creating something new out of something old. Consider the difficulty of reforming an institution's culture. Most reform efforts try to change people's attitudes and behaviors, and reformers are often surprised at how difficult that is. But when people with different interests can come together in a new setting—a safely neutral environment where ideals are shared, responsibility is equalized, and trust is created—breakthroughs can occur. The thinking of the whole group can have a powerful impact on individual members' environments as members gain partners who provide mutual support and encouragement.

Community building does not always immediately serve a college's purposes, but over the long term, benefits emerge in positive and often unforeseen ways. In the case of the air force base closure discussed in chapter 4, a difficult transformation of the facility provided an opportunity for participants from local school districts, community colleges, universities, businesses, and government to create a community educational center that has had a positive effect on their own operations.

Although there are specific effective methods for community building, success often goes beyond systematic procedure and technique: Trust, confidence, and setting aside self-interest play important roles. Any useful model for community building must include all of these components:

- Stakeholder commitment and interdependence
- Improved knowledge of each partner
- Shared values
- Expanded networks
- Achievement of shared goals

Community Building Is an Active Process

Most community colleges, by name and by general predisposition, already have community identities—even civic and local popularity. But community building as defined here is more activist in nature. It involves actively creating a community cluster, nurturing and sustaining it, and aligning it to a larger community that shares a common interest. Such shared interests can range widely, from healthcare reform, policy enactment, safety, preschool-through-college (P–16) initiatives, and crime, to dropout prevention, teacher training, school reform, and other objectives. As Marie Pepicello, former Phoenix College president, described the community-building process, "Part of the vision is that the community creates the vision."

The AACC Commission on the Future of Community Colleges' 1988 *Building Communities* report took community building beyond previous local and regional service characteristics, introducing such concepts as *learning communities* and foreshadowing the current literature on the topic. The report, though important, did not fully stress the activist nature of community building. We believe that a more proactive, systemic effort is needed. The late Ernest L. Boyer, an active member of the commission, stated that community colleges stand out among other higher-education institutions for being "the institution of engagement." Community building is a process of even deeper and more lasting engagement than the traditional—even innovative—course-related activities.

Rapidly changing forces are causing community colleges to rethink their roles. Community building in the 1960s, 1970s, and 1980s involved *getting* to the community; in this century, community colleges must strengthen and sustain communities by *being in* them. While community colleges have learned to meet workforce demands and university requirements, these are only some of the community needs they will need to meet in the 21st century if they are to help improve the quality of life and student preparedness.

Some recent examples of community building stand out:

- On September 11, 2001, Antonio Pérez, president of the Borough of Manhattan Community College in New York City, stood in his seventh-floor office and watched the attack on the World Trade Center. Only three blocks away, a community was being demolished before his eyes. This community included a branch college that was adjacent to 7 World Trade Center, a building that later collapsed. Within hours, the college's main campus had been transformed into a command center for the New York Fire and Police Departments, and emergency services were delivered from a site that had been a calm place of learning. The community college's mission was altered in a time of acute community need.

- During altercations between citizens and the Los Angeles Police Department after the Rodney King incident in March 1991, parts of the city were ablaze. The three Los Angeles Community College District institutions in the affected area were not harmed; instead, they became what Don Phelps, then the district's chancellor, referred to as "neutral places" where people came to rest, plan together, and feel safe.

- In 1989, many Haitian refugees fled to Miami, Florida, seeking political asylum and a safe haven for their families. Miami-Dade Community College (MDCC) provided them with access to human services and support agencies, distributing food, clothing, medical care, job information, shelter, and other life-saving services in the college's stadium. The college is also well known for the community spirit it demonstrated by helping area residents cope with the aftermath of Hurricane Hugo in 1994.

- Robert Todd, president of Oklahoma City Community College, transformed that institution into a crisis-relief center after a devastating tornado hit the community in 1999. The 210-mile-per-hour tornado was on the ground for nearly four hours. It wiped out 65 miles of homes, businesses, schools, and landscape, nearly leveling two communities. To meet immediate needs, Todd established an emergency shelter at the college. Faculty and students acted as brokers for supplies and communications. Within days, the college became a temporary home for displaced elementary and high school classes.

Communities must transform themselves and continuously renew their shared values. We believe that this kind of continuous renewal, strengthened by college and community dialogue, will help colleges respond to community crises and will assist college personnel when responsibilities and resources quickly change.

Making the Case for Community Building

Community building requires deep engagement and the sharing of common interests, resources, and values both within and beyond college walls. We make the case for community college participation in community building through the examples in this book, which support the following arguments:

Isolation Is Dangerous

Community colleges are in great peril when they are isolated from their communities. Not long ago, community colleges had simpler missions and stronger funding sources. Today, legislative and policy leaders have pushed community colleges into survival mode. Colleges and their communities now depend on shared resources and mutual, interdependent support. The colleges must know who is "out there"; it is no longer "them" and "us." As categorical funding disappears, block grants and state-formula funding will become the norm, greatly reducing the control and flexibility for locally driven programs.

Community building can increase a community college's options for funding. Corporate workforce training, which involves municipalities, small businesses, and neighborhoods, has eclipsed older vocational funding. Local school-reform initiatives have led community colleges to create after-school tutorials that are organized by college instructional designers and delivered at the Urban League or at a church community center. Health and human services program staff must look to locally based agencies, municipalities, state welfare departments, community-based organizations, and churches for alliances. This kind of creative thinking can lead to better recognition within the community, increasing community colleges' possible sources of financial support.

Institutions Must Understand Their Communities

Understanding the community outside its walls helps to define a community college's mission. Significant change in a college comes from adapting roles, rules, and responsibilities in accordance with real community needs. Rick Miller, past president of the Boys and Girls Clubs of Metropolitan Phoenix, says this:

> Social service providers and community volunteers start their work day as educators end theirs. Elementary students become children in need when school is out. College students become community volunteers to help keep kids off the streets. We are serving the same people, but we are not meeting all their needs; schools, colleges, and community groups haven't discovered how to work well together on their behalf.

Communities can help their colleges reconstruct themselves, which in turn allows colleges to manage forces that affect them, such as marketplace and enrollment trend pressures. A community college's most enduring values are to be found in its community.

Stakeholder Collaboratives Are Powerful

David Jacobson, a professor at New York University's Wagner School of Public Service, has written about the value of stakeholder collaboratives:

> The convergence towards team-based organization in schools, colleges, and workplaces creates both the need and the opportunity for communities to create two separate but overlapping partnerships of team-based organizations, what I call *Stakeholder Learning Collaboratives*. In this context, "stakeholder" emphasizes the important role multiple stakeholders play in organizational performance, including customers/clients,

suppliers, local communities, and especially employees. Employees have a stake in the performance of their teams, team members have a stake in the performance of other teams and in the overall performance of their organizations, and organizations have a stake in the performance of their external partners. (2001, 5–6)

Private industry has used stakeholder collaboratives in creative ways. For example, manufacturers organize suppliers, distributors, and retailers to optimize their effectiveness and improve service. Stakeholder collaboratives hold lessons for community colleges. The description of the Phoenix Think Tank's activities in chapter 4 illustrates how a community collaborative can serve the mutual interests of stakeholders.

All of these arguments are fueled by one powerful belief: Communities can become more resilient, and community colleges—in an activist role—can help them do so. Community-building initiatives can improve the life chances of youth and adults, expand hope, and foster self-sufficiency.

Should Community Colleges Have Social Agendas?

Arguments in favor of community building raise the question of whether community colleges should have social agendas, which can by no means be answered with one voice. The colleges get pulled this way and that by local politics. They are accountable to their own boards' mandates; to the agendas of mayors and other municipal leaders; and to their areas' special-interest groups, manpower commissions, and community-based organizations, which are fiercely competitive about prerogative and territory.

Policymakers are not always concerned with a social agenda. Most try to limit community college functions to core purposes and general education fundamentals. This posture is largely a reaction to employers' complaints that high school and even college graduates are unprepared for the workplace. Edmund J. Gleazer underscored the shortsightedness of this approach:

> Few policymakers seemed aware of the adult learner phenomenon and society's need for continuing education. Even more troubling, in all of my travels and conversations with legislators, governors, and state planners, seldom did I hear education acknowledged as a resource to be utilized in dealing with pressing societal needs such as mental health, corrections, unemployment, economic development, rising costs of health care, family disorganization, and energy conservation and development . . . .We need new and stronger coalitions of those who support education for improving the human condition. The views that unite us may be a good deal stronger than the turf problems that often divide us. (1995, 16–18)

Building alternative resources with many community collaborators may be the only way for community colleges to improve social conditions. Already, many socially useful programs have to be funded by limited resources. By joining forces with other institutions, colleges can maximize their ability to provide services ranging from assisting inner-city schools to helping families in crisis.

Community building is one way to carry out a community college's goal of being an integral part of the community, to define the purpose and values it has in common with the community, and to restructure the community support system for both students and citizens. For the good of the community and the good of the college, community colleges should understand and accept their social responsibility.

Chapter 2

Challenging the Obstacles to Community Building

Moving away from such core functions as university transfer, general education, technical offerings, and specialized career programs puts a community college at risk from policymakers and such threats as taxpayer revolts and cost-cutting referenda.

Authorities, Mandates, and Covenants

We examined the enabling statutes of community colleges in several states to determine how deep their mandates for community development are. Much of the legislation was enacted in the 1970s and 1980s, when community service, even in a broad sense, was not particularly in vogue.

Donald Puyear, the former executive director of the Arizona Board of Directors for Community Colleges, assisted us by polling several state directors of community college boards by e-mail. Puyear asked, "Does your state consider community development a part of the community college mission? If so, is there explicit statutory language to support that consideration?"

The findings, while not conclusive, were quite surprising: Few statutes include language that supports community development or community building as a central function of the community college. Connecticut's and Virginia's general statutes include well-developed model language that supports community building, but other statutes either do not support community building, or support it only weakly.

Colorado
Interviewed: Dorothy Horrell
Even though a number of Colorado colleges are actively involved in community development, it is not part the statutory role and mission.

Connecticut

Respondent: Andrew C. McKurdy

Section 10a-80 of the Connecticut General Statutes is clear and thorough, and could serve as a model for states that wish to mandate colleges' involvement with the community at a state level. The legislation is artfully written, providing clear justification for community-building programs. It also specifies that colleges should not be altered by community activities.

Sec. 10a-80. (Formerly Sec. 10-381). Community service programs at regional community-technical colleges.

The primary responsibilities of the regional community-technical colleges shall be

(1) to provide programs of occupational, vocational, technical and technological and career education designed to provide training for immediate employment, job retraining or upgrading of skills to meet individual, community and state manpower needs;

(2) to provide programs of general study, including, but not limited to, remediation, general and adult education and continuing education designed to meet individual student goals;

(3) to provide programs of study for college transfer representing the first two years of baccalaureate education;

(4) to provide community service programs as defined in subsection (b) of this section and

(5) to provide student support services including, but not limited to, admissions, counseling, testing, placement, individualized instruction and efforts to serve students with special needs. . . .

(b) As used in this section, "community service programs" means educational, cultural, recreational and community directed services which a community-technical college may provide in addition to its regular academic program.

Such community service programs may include, but shall not be limited to

(1) activities designed to enrich the intellectual, cultural and social life of the community,

(2) educational services designed to promote the development of skills for the effective use of leisure time,

(3) activities and programs designed to assist in the identification and solution of community problems and

(4) utilization of college facilities and services by community groups to the extent such usage does not conflict with the regular schedule of the college.

Idaho

Respondent: Mike Killworth

"[The] Idaho statute concerning community colleges in the state does not specifically address community development. The connection between education/training opportunities and community development/ building is welcome. The board strategic plan, in a general way, addresses community development and community building."

Maine

Respondent: Ellyn Chase

Maine does not have a community college system. The technical colleges in Maine in many ways serve that function. However, there is nothing in Maine's statutes that speaks to community development, although all of our technical colleges are very actively involved in their communities and regions.

Oklahoma

Respondent: Hans Brisch

Oklahoma does not have statutory language supporting this portion of the mission of two-year colleges. The state regents, however, have constitutional authority for determining the function of institutions.

Although the function assignment for the two-year colleges could be more sharply stated in this regard, it does provide, among other things, for the two-year colleges to

- provide both formal and informal programs of study especially designed for adults and out-of-school youth in order to serve the community generally with a continuing education opportunity;
- participate in programs of economic development with comprehensive or regional universities toward the end that the needs of each institution's geographic service area are met.

Virginia

Respondent: Joy Graham

Three subsections of the Virginia code outline community colleges' responsibility for community relationships fairly clearly:

- to enrich local communities, by making available resources in people, facilities, libraries, and programming;
- to take a leadership role in helping shape the future direction of their communities;
- to enhance economic, cultural, and educational partnerships between the colleges and the communities they serve.

Although Virginia's statutory support is not as extensive as Connecticut's, its mandate that community colleges "take a leadership role in helping shape the future direction of their communities" supports community building more than most other state statutes do.

Arizona and MCCD

Arizona's statutes mention only three functions for community colleges: transfer education, technical education, and vocational education. The vision and mission statements in the *Maricopa Community College District Policy Manual* (1999) barely touch on community responsibility:

Vision:

The Maricopa Community Colleges strive to exceed the changing expectations of our many communities for effective, innovative, student-centered, flexible, and lifelong educational opportunities. Our employees are committed to respecting diversity, continuous quality improvement, and the efficient use of resources. We are a learning organization guided by our shared values.

Mission:

The Maricopa Community Colleges create and continuously improve affordable, accessible, effective, and safe learning environments for the lifelong educational needs of the diverse communities we serve. Our colleges fulfill the mission through: University Transfer Education, General Education, Developmental Education, Workforce Development, Student Development Services, Continuing Education, and Community Education.

MCCD crafted these statements in Strategic Conversations that included community members. In the vision statement, the word *community* refers only to MCCD's attempts to meet the expectations of the community. It does not refer to the system's role in addressing the community's nonacademic and unidentified needs, even as they affect current and future students. Although MCCD's mission statement names seven specific ways in which the colleges will fulfill their mission, it does not address community building specifically.

Stealth Functions

We found little legal support, no funding support, and some risk involved for community colleges who become involved in community building. Donald Puyear's interviews suggest that, except in a few states, community colleges have not sought authority for community development from their state statutes. As Puyear puts it, colleges have seen involvement in community education or community development as a *stealth function*—a function that has little legal backing and minimal or no financing.

MCCD, like many of the nation's community colleges, has a number of stealth functions that are not specifically spelled out in its charter or enabling legislation. David R. Pierce, former president of the American Association of Community Colleges, reminds us that although all community colleges provide remedial education, few state statutes for community colleges mention it. Other examples of stealth functions include welfare-reform efforts and intervening in schools.

Welfare Reform

Many of the roles played by community colleges have been determined by federal and state mandates that fall outside the boundaries of the colleges' original state enabling laws. For example, in the area of welfare reform, the Personal Responsibility and Work Opportunity Reconciliation Act (PRWORA) of 1996 pushed community colleges into providing human services, an area of conflicting and sometimes self-defeating interests. Some community colleges already had significant numbers of welfare recipients enrolled in their programs. In some states, community colleges were designated as preferred providers, while in others they were expected to compete with preferred providers. Many community colleges hoped to educate welfare recipients in a way that emphasized work preparation and personal support, but PRWORA administrators insisted that they instead put those students to work—period.

Many community college personnel felt they had an understanding of the welfare community, and many community college students had marginal, if not poverty-level, incomes. Many of those who promulgated federal and state rules were ignorant of the work community colleges do, but those who worked in the colleges knew who the welfare recipients were: our neighbors, nephews, cousins, and students. Long before welfare reform, community colleges had a role in many programs that affected these peoples' lives.

Welfare reform did bring community colleges to the policy table on the critical national problem of chronic welfare recipients. A policy paper published by the Education Commission of the States (Allen 1998) reviews the track record of community colleges in assisting poverty-level students:

> Many community colleges have become skilled in the delivery of programs especially designed to overcome the education barriers faced by low-income students. . . . Community colleges and state community college systems have sometimes partnered with local and state social service departments to serve welfare recipients. Especially when other options are limited, community colleges may become the social service departments' preferred providers. In other cases, community colleges compete for welfare students against nonprofit agencies and proprietary schools offering comparable short-term training. . . . The enactment of welfare reform, the Personal Responsibility and Work Opportunity Reconciliation Act of 1996, is having a significant impact on the role of community colleges in the education of welfare recipients. (1)

Many community college leaders believe that federal policymakers do not grasp the colleges' knowledge of their communities. Those who wish to enhance this understanding will be hard put to find financing, legal basis, or even recognition by policymakers of a proven community role.

Intervening in the Schools

Another way that community colleges support community development is by working with the secondary and elementary schools in their areas. Officials in Virginia understand that many social ills and community problems are manifested in the plight of the schools, and that state's code lists this as a legitimate function, but in most states it is a stealth function, not supported by legislation.

The Maricopa Community Colleges, LaGuardia Community College in New York, and other pioneers of middle-college and alternative high school experiences have found that the healthiest communities have the healthiest schools. MCCD has learned the value of collaborating with community agencies to address system maladies present among the school populations.

Collaborating with elementary and secondary schools in its area alerted MCCD to community needs: When MCCD asked school counselors and principals what their priorities were, the immediate response was, "We need family support centers!" In most jurisdictions, no larger authority gives community colleges either the legal mandate or the funding to serve the community this way, so this kind of community building and development is indeed a stealth function that is more likely to be locally conceived and driven than it is to come from a state or regional level. But, authorities and mandates may help to clarify the different levels of support for community development work and explain why community colleges in some places have quite robust community agendas while others engage in very little community work.

Internal Tensions

Community colleges may themselves be undecided about their community-building mission. Board and faculty members and administrative and staff leaders all play a role in clarifying how a college will engage in community building and who will be responsible for community-building activities. Lack of support from any of these stakeholders can make a college's community-building efforts fail, so it is important to address an institution's internal tensions about community building.

From 1992 to 1994, as a part of the Beacon College Project designed by AACC and supported by the W. K. Kellogg Foundation, MCCD conducted a national survey of community colleges regarding their community-building activities. Findings showed a growing interest in community building among CEOs; however, a majority of respondents indicated they were not confident in their ability to lead the effort. A majority of college managers reported a variety of partnerships for direct support to students, but few had formed *coalitions* with the goal of improving long-range collaborative relationships with their community.

Strategic Conversations

At MCCD, community building resulted from multiple discussions among concerned parties and from agenda setting by active leadership. At first, some board members opposed both the principle of community building and specific programs. To their credit, board members, administrators, and faculty aired their differing points of view in several sessions called Strategic Conversations. These open sessions usually included the presentation of a background paper, a facilitated discussion, and a proposal for further study or action. Members of the community gave presentations during some of the sessions. These conversations let participants learn more about community building by giving them background information, letting them examine their motives, and clarifying their points of agreement and disagreement.

In April 1996, MCCD conducted a Strategic Conversation with communities in the Phoenix metropolitan area, using the theme "Building Communities: Listening and Learning Together." The conversation, lasting two and a half hours, took place at GateWay Community College. Planning and research–committee members from each of the 10 MCCD colleges attended. A background paper provided a brief overview of collaborative programs and activities underway among colleges and their neighboring schools, universities, and community organizations.

Some of the collaboratives outlined took the form of community coalitions with long-range plans for systemic change. For the purpose of the conversation, *coalition* was defined as a structured organization of collaborating people representing a broad range of organizations or individuals who share a commitment to a particular mission. In a 1996 survey, MCCD colleges listed 32 different programs as community-building activities beyond academic services.

At Strategic Conversations, board members and CEOs sat with college and community participants, following a "no rank in the room" policy. Facilitators led small discussion groups and posted the notes from the sessions on the college's e-mail system for all employees to read. The recommendations that came out of the conversations became part of the board's agendas.

Mesa Community College, the largest of the MCCD institutions, held its community-building discussions over a two-year period. Mesa's fall 2001 convocation for employees opened with a focus on community building, which was to be a yearlong theme. A speaker addressed the topic, and a faculty-staff panel followed with comments. In addition, the college formally added "community building" to its values statement.

When there is lack of consensus about a college's community-building efforts, there is no better remedy than informed, sensible, civil discourse. Strategic Conversations are an effective way to create support for community building, as are student dialogues and community symposiums.

Striving for Balance

MCCD continues to struggle with internal tensions about its roles and priorities in regard to community building. While complex social issues call for community awareness and a community development strategy, other voices often command the attention of leaders. MCCD is faced with the fundamental challenge of carrying out an urban-based social agenda with scarce resources, lack of enthusiastic support from state-level policy shapers, and its own internal lack of agreement about mission and purpose.

MCCD must both meet the community's rising social demands and serve its region's economic development needs. These forces create a dynamic tension in the MCCD system. Conversations with college presidents and chancellors in RC-2000, AACC, and other meetings bear out that these same forces affect community colleges throughout the United States and other parts of the world. Unlike institutions that have clearly defined roles that are independent of their communities, America's community colleges mold themselves to fit their communities.

Partnerships, Coalitions, and Collaboratives

We distinguish levels of community involvement according to the following general definitions, developed in the early 1990s during the AACC–W. K. Kellogg Foundation Beacon College Project.

Partnership: Usually a short-term relationship or activity that may be formed for a specific program or grant opportunity. Although not all partners will stay the course long enough to become collaborators, they may pave the way for others to work productively for a longer time.

Coalition: Has a broader mission and longer time line than a partnership (more than five years). Serves a broad mission to improve a system and, in the case of workshops, to build relationships that will stay connected even during times of no funding, no specific program, and no supervisory directive. Coalitions may also include partnerships working on specific projects within the larger membership base.

Collaborative: Similar to a coalition. In addition, collaborators look for opportunities to fulfill the mission—they are "dream makers." Collaborators may be visionaries, planners, researchers, fundraisers, and note takers. After determining community needs and matching them with talents and interests of members, they work together as an efficient team, striving to work at a mature level that avoids power play, competition, and turf protection.

Chapter 3

Micro-Community Development

This chapter discusses strategies used in the Phoenix area for effective *micro-community development*—that is, community building at the most local level, often the neighborhood.

Contradictions in Phoenix

It has been said that all politics are local. A national or state government can be visionary, effective, and popular, but if it does not favorably affect local communities and life in the neighborhoods, it is to a certain extent irrelevant. In the late 1970s and early 1980s, Phoenix, Arizona, developed a promising model for local neighborhood development. Under the leadership of Mayor Terry Goddard, the city government created multiple commissions to serve the city's "villages"—specific planning zones that corresponded to existing neighborhoods. The Phoenix Planning Commission provided the village commissions with strategic guidance and technical and research services. Although many of the commissions were understaffed, they performed their planning duties eagerly and earnestly, lodging recommendations on quality of life, transportation integration, mixed-use land development, education, community service, and other planning issues with the city planning commission.

At the time, Phoenix was undergoing vigorous growth. Development surged in the outer corridors of the city (such as the Camelback corridor and Scottsdale) and the financial firms and retail operations that had been in the central city dispersed to those outer corridors, leaving Phoenix unable to maintain a viable downtown. Desperate to stop the dispersal, the city permitted large office buildings to be built along parts of the central avenue corridor, with disastrous results for some of the village commissions and their neighborhoods. Parking structures to support the new buildings were built just off the central corridor, and some streets dead-ended to accommodate them. Other neighborhood streets became one-way arterials, preventing residents from parking or conveniently approaching their homes. Charming cottages were overshadowed by their new concrete neighbors, large residential areas were condemned, and old downtown neighborhoods were frequently lost to the bulldozer.

Communities throughout the United States have instituted planning policies similar to Phoenix's decision to permit large-scale development in the central city. Such policies constitute a kind of violence against neighborhoods that can be as destructive and long lasting as criminal violence. To protect themselves, neighborhoods need help from partnerships and coalitions that look out for their special local interests.

Grant Park

In Phoenix, downtown Grant Park was a center of pickup basketball games, picnics, and neighborhood events, and it served as one of the focal points of the community. The community had no open green area beyond the park. Then Arizona's largest public utility placed a row of transformers and insulators, some as tall as 20 feet, at one end of the park, making the park's most visible feature a cyclone-fenced enclosure of massive transformers and wires. Community members were neither consulted nor informed about this drastic change before it happened. The trucks and cranes just moved in one morning, and the placement of the transformers went unchallenged until it was too late.

It is extremely unlikely that city planners would choose to locate an installation like this one in a wealthier neighborhood, where citizens would probably balk. Resistance in one community usually causes planners to look for less-resistant communities where the residents are less informed, less educated, and less powerful. In the case of the Grant Park utility installation, the park's neighbors were the victims of a kind of planning violence because city leaders placed less value on their poorer community than they would have on another.

South Phoenix

South Phoenix is another example. For years this area south of the Salt River went without emergency medical centers. Until an ABCO supermarket came to the neighborhood in 1997, the city's downtown residents—many of whom were newly arrived immigrants from Mexico and other countries—did not have convenient access to a large grocery store. Since many had no transportation, they had to buy such staples as milk, bread, fruit, and canned goods from an expensive convenience store. In this case, the absence of mixed neighborhood planning meant that the historic downtown neighborhood lacked essential services, something that could have been prevented if the community had been developed through a broader, more powerful community partnership or coalition.

Strategies in Inner Cities

Two micro-community development projects in Phoenix's inner city stand out: the Garcia Neighborhood Project, which did not involve the Maricopa Community College District but which influenced MCCD's future community-building philosophy; and Neighborhood College, which involved MCCD's Phoenix College.

The Garcia Neighborhood Project

Phoenix's West Van Buren community lies west of the downtown Phoenix commercial and government corridor. Its residents are largely Hispanic, but other immigrants live in the area, which offers relatively inexpensive housing. Named after a major commercial street, West Van Buren is full of dilapidated motels, strips of small businesses, and auto repair and parts shops. Small bungalow homes in multiblock patches surround industrial warehouses, salvage yards, and mixed industrial/commercial areas. A huge freeway expansion with multiple interchange stacks strangles the community. West Van Buren had been the epicenter of drug trade and prostitution since the mid-1970s.

Children, of course, suffer in such an environment. Teachers who see children come to school dirty or bruised are in a quandary: Should they refer a child to Child Protective Services? Once a family is referred it can take months for it to get help, and trying to get proper help for a child can tie up teachers and administrators for days.

In 1988, Bob Donofrio became superintendent of the Murphy Elementary School District, which serves the children of West Van Buren. Donofrio, who had been a human-services provider before becoming a superintendent, began to take action, requesting that the Arizona State Department of Economic Security (DES) place health and human services intake technicians in his district. Before long, a dozen human-services workers had uncovered systemic community patholo-gies. In response, DES established counseling and referral services for families in crisis in the schools. These services provided support for school faculty who were confronted with evidence of abuse or other home crises.

With the assistance of other neighborhood figures, Donofrio helped take back the community from the criminals, drug peddlers, addicts, and prostitutes. Industry owners, business leaders, churches, community-based organizations, and the schools sought to clean up Van Buren Avenue. The police department added driving and walking patrols. An action group—including educators, parents, business owners, city council representatives, and neighborhood association leaders—organized Neighborhood Watch programs and Mothers Against Gangs, a community cooperative, to devise a strategy to curtail gang recruitment. Safety brigades helped the elderly shop and pick up prescriptions. The Holsum

Bakery staff volunteered for community cleanup, painting, and graffiti-removal projects. Edward Eisele, the bakery's third-generation owner, who was a member of the influential Phoenix 40 business group, coordinated many initiatives. Thanks to all these activities, the community's ownership of the streets and neighborhoods was restored.

The Garcia Neighborhood Project was Phoenix's best systemic model of micro-community rebuilding. Eisele attempted with some success to get members of the Phoenix 40 to set up similar projects in other regions of the city. The Phoenix 40's greatest efforts were to employ inner-city youth over the summer and after school and to explore community issues by setting up forums and committees to analyze community drug, crime, and gang problems.

That effort provided the colleges with valuable lessons in how to support students' families. As discussed in chapter 4, the Phoenix Think Tank used those lessons to establish several Family Resource Centers, where students and their families receive healthcare, mentoring, recreational activities, tutoring, and parent education. The goal is to help children and youth in school—whatever it takes.

Neighborhood College

Phoenix College is located in central Phoenix. In the one-and-a-half-mile radius around it, fewer than one-third of the households are traditional two-parent households; instead, most are headed either by an elderly person or by a (usually female) single parent. In 1994, the college established close ties with the Osborn Elementary School District, in particular with the nearby Longview Elementary School. The college and the schools undertook a neighborhood assessment process that identified many needs, including the need for financial planning for those with limited incomes.

Phoenix College offered to be a connecting point for neighborhood organizations that address citizen needs and created the Neighborhood

College, which took on various forms and became an important catalyst for service to the community. Phoenix College's then-president, Marie Pepicello, offered college resources including duplicating, mail labeling, and e-mail service to neighborhood leaders, and community leaders including an MCCD board member and a city councilman advised Pepicello on the project. Among other things, the Neighborhood College trained homeowners association leaders in the basics of association management, conflict resolution, and influencing political decisions that affected their communities.

Strategies for Smaller Cities

Neighborhoods in larger urban areas are not the only places that need connectivity and solutions. Smaller cities also face their share of challenges. In addition to its community-building efforts in Phoenix, MCCD provided leadership for four initiatives in smaller cities.

Estrella Mountain Citizens' Academy

To help empower the local citizenry, the staff at Estrella Mountain Community College (EMCC), one of MCCD's newest colleges, developed the Southwest Valley Citizen Leadership Academy. The small cities of Avondale, Goodyear, Litchfield Park, Buckeye, and Tolleson select up-and-coming leaders—50 at a time—to learn how city government works. City managers, finance directors, council members, and other government insiders teach seven classes offered at the college. Through the academy, potential community leaders learn about the issues and the policies that affect them and how other city officials and citizens are handling them. They also learn how to plan, hold meetings, and react effectively to policies and politics. The community college acts as host and facilitator, not as instructor.

The program's regional approach to shared learning has made local citizens aware of resources and local experts. The participating towns have had a history of competing with and distrusting one another. The program gives their leaders the opportunity to look at the towns' common needs. Estrella Mountain Community College hosts most of the Academy's local and regional civic meetings and activities on its campus. According to EMCC's community education and community services director, Clay Goodman, "Each community has a need for more informed citizenry to serve on planning and zoning commissions. Homeowners groups [as a result of the academy] are assuming more responsibility for code enforcement that aligns with city policies."

Guadalupe Education Center

Guadalupe is a community of a few square blocks in the southeast corner of metropolitan Phoenix, sandwiched between two large freeways that hide its rustic beauty from passing commuters. Those who drive on the neighborhood's potholed streets see architecture that reflects old Mexico and hear various languages spoken. Most of the residents are non–English speaking, poor, and have either Yaqui tribal or Hispanic heritage.

Guadalupe is cut off from educational and economic success. MCCD's governing board became aware of the need for education in this area. With leadership from South Mountain Community College, the Guadalupe Education Center opened in 2000 as the first educational establishment in this small community. South Mountain College continues to operate the center at its parent campus.

The center's programs are staffed and financed by the Yaqui tribe, the citizens of Guadalupe, South Mountain Community College, and several community organizations, including the Boys and Girls Clubs. The center is growing in popularity among neighborhood residents, who appreciate the opportunities created by this collaborative effort. With its strong grassroots foundation of trust and understanding, Guadalupe Education Center is an excellent example of micro-community development.

Leadership in Scottsdale

All communities need leaders to advance. In 1986, Scottsdale Community College president Art Decabooter responded to the turnover in leadership in the Scottsdale area by setting up a leadership program on his campus. The 10-month program exposes local citizens to a broad range of topics including education, arts, human services, business, and government. Program graduates are recruited by employers and political leaders for key positions in the community.

The college has taken leadership training a step further with its Summer Youth Leadership Program for junior and senior high school students from the Salt River Community, a reservation of Pima tribal citizens. The program offers concurrent enrollment at the college, with a focus on the Pima language and culture. The program helps students assimilate into the nonreservation culture by helping them understand how their ancestry relates to their future opportunities.

Serving the Pima students is especially appropriate because the college sits on Pima-owned land. Decabooter also established a policy that allows all Pima tribal members to take classes free. Scottsdale Community College does not just sit in its community—its staff actively seeks to solve community problems. Faculty member Irwin Noyes says, "We pay the salary for a person to be in the community so that we can respond to the needs of the community, when and where people need us."

Mesa Connectors

Mesa Community College's Connectors program meets a simple micro-community need. In partnership with the Mesa Fire Department, the college provides selected students with a three-day orientation in what it means to be a *connector* in the community. Following this training in communication and social issues, students are stationed for four to six hours a week at the local fire station, where they provide on-call support to firefighters, cleaning up after fires, comforting victims, and helping victims find food, clothing, and housing.

Fire departments get major alarm calls, but they also get calls of a less serious nature. For example, a call might involve an elderly person who cannot reach his walker or who has misplaced her prescription pills or glasses. The student volunteers of the Connectors program respond to such calls, providing a remedy, resolution, or referral.

This valuable volunteering experience also builds a foundation for students to continue supporting their community. In this fast-paced world, it is easy for people to lose touch with others and lack a sense of community. The Connectors program builds hope and community goodwill. We point it out for its simplicity and because, despite its small scale, several programs have emanated from it. These include the Into the Streets project, through which Chandler-Gilbert, GateWay, and Mesa Community Colleges have provided more than 125 social service agencies with student volunteers. Connections like these are the building blocks of micro-community development.

Chapter 4

Macro-Community Development

In contrast to micro-community development—community development at the local level—*macro-community development* refers to initiatives that involve larger areas or regions. In Maricopa County, the Phoenix Think Tank, the East Valley Think Tank, the West Valley Think Tank, and Learning Connections in the north valley are large coalitions that involve numerous college, school, university, and community partners (see Figure 4.1). All are excellent examples of how a community college can play a powerful and effective role as a convening partner. One of the major features of these initiatives is collaboration among local schools, the Maricopa Community College District colleges, universities, and community organizations. College personnel take an active leadership role; the college president or the president's designee cochairs the coalition along with a school superintendent or business leaders. Each of the participating colleges has built a high level of trust and credibility among its peer members.

A Case Study—The Phoenix Think Tank

The Phoenix Think Tank (PTT) is a coalition of preschool-through-16 (P–16) and urban community interests. Membership on the Steering Committee includes 13 elementary school districts, a large high school district, five community colleges, three universities, government agencies, community-based organizations (CBO), and businesses. MCCD acts as convener and offers staff support for the group's operations and programs.

The Ford Foundation's national Urban Partnerships Program supported PTT from 1992 to 2002. In 1992, the Business Higher-Education Forum awarded PTT its Anderson Medal for "building educational excellence through an exemplary business–higher education–public

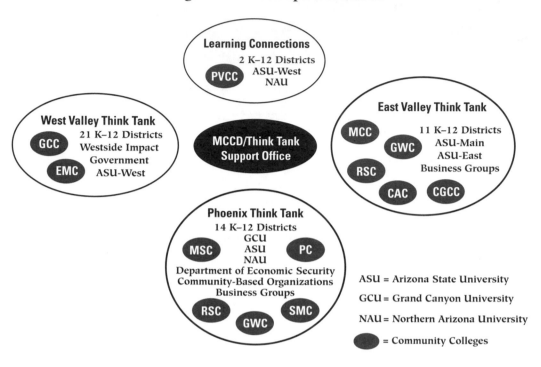

Figure 4.1 Maricopa Coalitions

school alliance." In 1998, the League for Innovation in the Community College selected MCCD and the PTT to be one of three sites for a large national demonstration project. In 1998, MCCD's chancellor and PTT's founder were awarded the McGraw-Hill Prize for demonstrating educational excellence in community building.

As Go the Schools, So Goes the City

The Phoenix Think Tank was created in 1988 after Timothy Dyer, then superintendent of the Phoenix Union High School District, issued a warning: "As go the schools, so goes the city." By the mid-1980s, serious problems were emerging behind the pristine resorts and golf courses of the beautiful desert city of Phoenix. Key business leaders had plans for the city to become the next Silicon Valley and were demanding more school accountability. Local chambers of commerce were recruiting corporate headquarters to move to the Phoenix Valley of the Sun. Business startups were increasing at about 8 percent per year. The entrepreneurs who established businesses in the city in response to enticement packages assumed that they would find the trained workers they needed. Instead, they found an inadequate workforce. Phoenix's school system was recognizing a high number of dropouts and an even larger number of high school graduates who were unprepared for college or employment. Meanwhile, the city's growing per capita crime rate had surpassed those of New York City and Miami. Superintendent Dyer's words rang true: The city was heading in the same direction as the schools. Several community leaders heard this wakeup call.

The Phoenix metropolitan area has 57 school districts, 14 of them serving urban students. Each district has its own superintendent, budget, governing board, educational policies, and priorities. In the inner city, the 13 elementary school districts send their graduates to Phoenix high schools. The feeder pattern was complex, with some elementary schools delivering students to as many as four different high schools and little tracking of students into postsecondary school. A stronger communication link was needed to build a seamlessness among P–16 institutions.

By the mid-1980s, there had been years of little communication or coordination among the different districts. Resources were misappropriated and students were frequently lost in the system. In 1995, one elementary school principal said he could not find any of his 85 students in any high school two years after they had graduated from the eighth grade. Because available data were inadequate and often misinterpreted, no one really knew how many students were dropping out. This situation had developed not from lack of caring by school personnel but from a lack of staff time needed for follow-through. Another part of the problem was that the agencies and colleges near the schools acted as if the schools' problems did not exist. The colleges seemed to believe that those were school problems, not their problems.

In response to these difficulties, Superintendent Dyer and Paul Elsner, then chancellor of MCCD, formed the Phoenix Think Tank, whose mission was to share the resources and thinking of all stakeholders so that students would enter, reenter, and remain in education until their maximum learning potential and goals could be achieved. Shortly thereafter, MCCD created the Think Tank Department (TTD) to support PTT and Maricopa's 10 community colleges in their community-building efforts. The governing board members helped to support the efforts by adding a budget amount to provide operational support and by writing a job description for a director position. The job description may be summarized as follows:

1. Direct and support the activities of a K–16 community coalition (the PTT).
2. Assist community colleges in Maricopa County, Arizona, and the nation to establish or expand K–16 community consortia.
3. Shape the political dialogue surrounding education at the city, county, state, and national levels.
4. Assist to position the coalition and the Maricopa Community College District to maintain educational currency locally and nationally.
5. Maintain liaison with program officers of foundations and education associations with an emphasis on maintaining strong local and national networks.
6. Direct all aspects of RC-2000, a national federation of the largest community colleges in the United States and other countries.

Governance, Directive, and Funding

From the beginning, PTT programs and activities were funded with outside grants and contributions secured by staff and coalition members. To prevent the PTT from competing with local schools or college foundations for scarce resources, most of the funding came from national sources. Since its inception, approximately $24 million has come from external grants and $4 million from MCCD and other PTT members.

Partnerships with other organizations provided the PTT with extensive in-kind contributions and shared resources. Release time for university faculty, the use of community college facilities, loaned business executives, and donated equipment are just a few of the contributions that have sustained coalition activities. About 25 percent of the money collected was given directly to teachers or schools to support self-improvement efforts. The rest has been used for large-scale training, team development, research, evaluation, and networking events to build capacity to improve both the schools' and the communities' ability to improve services and student support.

The leaders of the PTT agreed that it would be counterproductive to issue top-down directives or mandates to schools or colleges. Instead, the CEOs from each of the member institutions acted as conceptualizers and enablers to support the projects created by staff and community volunteers—mostly from midmanagement levels—who took responsibility to sustain the collaborative work.

Steps in the Phoenix Think Tank Development

As the Phoenix Think Tank evolved and its participants developed mutual comfort, respect, and understanding, they became productive as team members with a common goal. Their steps in developing as a team toward a common goal are as follows:

Step 1: Affiliation. In PTT's early months of design beginning in January 1989, members became acquainted, overcoming geographical differences and beginning to learn about each other's needs, talents, and available services. One of the most valuable activities was to have principals and education specialists describe their programs to an external audience of businesses and community associations. This activity built affinity between educators and other community stakeholders who had been critical of school failures, perceiving the schools to be inefficient. Teachers began to see college staff as credible potential partners. When the schools talked about eighth-grade algebra readiness, the community college math teachers recognized the similarity to their own challenge. The schools discovered that MCCD had been offering community-wide parenting classes for years, and the colleges learned about the school districts' plans for parent programs and teacher development.

By the second meeting of the Phoenix Union High School and MCCD staffs, the PTT effort was expanded to include five of the feeder elementary school districts and Arizona State University. During a two-year development period, PTT members came to know each other as dedicated people who worked long hours to improve conditions for students. They also learned a great deal about school issues—including school reform, educational restructuring, and systematic change—through guest speakers and monthly dialogues.

As issues were discussed and data analyzed among the broader community, PTT members, some of whom had been critics of the schools, came to appreciate what the schools had to deal with: family crises, poverty, student illiteracy, student apathy, limited staff, large classrooms, limited materials, and absent parents.

PTT members compiled and studied the compelling data:

- Elementary school districts were approaching 70 to 80 percent minority enrollment.
- The high school four-year dropout rate was over 45 percent, the second highest in the nation.
- Phoenix high schools had an epidemic of teen pregnancy.
- The average birth weight of babies born to teenage mothers was 4.5 pounds.
- Gang membership was soaring as Los Angeles gangs relocated

to the Phoenix area and promised students personal support and a sense of identity.

- Growing numbers of single-parent families were providing less personal and academic support for their children.
- Students were less academically prepared and the number of non-English-speaking students had increased as the result of immigration from Mexico and other parts of Latin America.
- School violence was increasing.
- Student unrest and lack of self-discipline interfered with learning.

Dyer continued to stress that when schools decline, their cities become weaker. He then took a next step—training motivated presenters who gave slide presentations to the community at every opportunity. Rotary clubs, chambers of commerce, senior citizen groups, the Board of Regents who govern Arizona's three state universities, parent-teacher organizations, and the media were some of the recipients of PTT's message. This got the community's attention, but the PTT still needed to clarify what was to be done. Toward this end, the governing board members came together to talk about issues of community-wide importance. MCCD governing board member Linda B. Rosenthal invited elected school board members, members of the Board of Regents, and leaders of business-community organizations to single-theme dinner meetings that provided time to socialize and strategize. The goal was to make the members aware of the problems common to their institutions. No solutions were adopted right away, but each participant was invited to join a solution team, under the general heading of "Skunkworks." Giving these leaders firsthand information and the opportunity to ask questions in the early stages of PTT's development helped make the later institutionalization of programs and services stronger.

Step 2: Positioning. With the understanding that collaboration might be foreign to those who had worked in isolation for years, key organizers within the member institutions participated in a series of workshops, dialogues, and team-building retreats. From January 1992 to September 1994, more than 350 volunteers had taken part in the workshops and were actively leading PTT's initiatives. In academia, rewards, promotions, and tenure were commonly awarded on the basis of independent research, teaching, or program management. The education curriculum provided little or no training in collaboration strategies. Changing PTT's participants from independent to interdependent was a time-consuming task, but an important one to complete before beginning work on projects.

The PTT Steering Committee—made up of the CEOs of member institutions—met monthly during this developmental stage and identified the following basic premises:

- PTT's members needed a place to come together and think.
- Maricopa County students facing adversity were not "somebody else's" students, they were everyone's students, whether they attended preschool, elementary school, middle school, high school, community college, or university.
- If enough time was devoted to real thinking and sharing of ideas, dedicated people could devise uncommon solutions to common problems.

The creation of the PTT collaborative had to compete with other priorities. This was a volunteer effort; there were no mandates or policies requiring participation. The participants had to have a personal desire to make the effort. They were all encouraged to align their personal values with the coalition's goals as they accepted PTT stewardship.

As the discussions proceeded, community college personnel were shocked to discover the beleaguered state of the city's schools. State agencies and the legislature were not providing the schools with the support they needed, and inner-city teachers were leaving the profession in great numbers because they lacked the financial, safety, and moral support enjoyed by their suburban school counterparts.

Community-wide brainstorming sessions produced hundreds of ideas. A research firm conducted a Best Practices Study to learn which programs helped students stay in and succeed in school. The PTT created a Development Team to further develop the suggestions and to find resources to support them. The coalition membership, now positioned for action, accepted responsibility for implementing projects.

Step 3: Partnering. By 1994, the collaborative was evolving, and school-reform movements were underway in the conservative business community. Tension in early PTT discussions came from business leaders' perception that high school graduates lacked the skills and knowledge needed for employment in the new knowledge- and technology-based economy. At first, the schools were encouraged by the business community's interest. Later, after hundreds of hours of dialogue, the school representatives became discouraged because they could not convince the business community that public schools could reform themselves if given financial support and encouragement.

The Phoenix Think Tank was the only group in Arizona at that time that had brought educators and business leaders together to talk and listen to one another. Although community college staff maintained an amicable relationship with local businesses (many of which were customers for the colleges' workforce training), their allegiance was to the schools. Under pressure from the business group, K–16 education leaders developed a stronger bond and a closer working relationship with one another and came together in a more determined unity.

During a 1994 summer retreat in Prescott, Arizona, PTT redesigned its structure into three working groups:

- The 21 CEOs from participating organizations expanded the **Steering Committee** (cochaired by MCCD's chancellor and the superintendent of one of the inner-city school districts) that focused on conceptualizing and enabling active solutions to overcome problems. In the early days, the group's leadership rotated. Participants agreed on a mission, designed a strategic plan, studied data, planned, and advertised their activities. In time, members became champions for selected projects, helping with fundraising, sharing resources, and accepting the responsibility for this new institution that would reflect the opinions and priorities of its members.

- The CEOs on the Steering Committee appointed trusted members of their institutions to a **Development Team** that would become the catalyst for implementation efforts. These team members became internal promoters, resource recruiters, implementers, and evaluators.

- A third group, the **Implementation Team**, which included K–12 teachers, community college and university faculty, students, parents, and community-based program managers, oversaw activities in the schools and community. The PTT philosophy was that those closest to students should help make the decisions that would affect them. This team collected and analyzed data, offered insights for making improvements to the schools, and assisted with program implementation.

Members of all three teams participate in an annual all-team meeting, a summer retreat, and various activities and social events. This participation has led to greater trust, better delegation of tasks, increased mutual respect, and the recognition of special leadership talents at all levels, as team members assert "the experts are among us." An all-day workshop called Visioning and Values, led by an outside facilitator, took team members through a process to identify and prioritize personal values and to align those values with PTT's mission and purpose. This activity led to a highly committed PTT team and strengthened the relationships among team members. Appendix D shows the list of values used as a basis for the dialogue.

Step 4: Coalition. When people from schools, colleges, community organizations, and government agencies work together effectively for several years, the chance for better learning environments improves. In 1992, the Phoenix Think Tank received competitive grants from both the Ford Foundation and The Pew Charitable Trusts to support the data gathering and planning that the coalition needed in order to act. The Pew funds were used to collect and analyze baseline data on all of Phoenix's K–12 inner-city schools. Researchers collected, analyzed, charted, and reported on more than 85 variables. The Ford Foundation funding was used for team development, with almost 350 people in 10 teams converting the data into action plans and programs for students and teachers.

Three additional functional teams were created to focus on research and evaluation, public relations, and community resources. Arizona State University's three campuses became more involved, as did community colleges, several community-based organizations, the state Department of Economic Security, the City of Phoenix, and the Arizona Alliance of Business, a network of individuals from new and evolving businesses. Four of the urban MCCD colleges took an active role: Rio Salado College; Phoenix College; South Mountain Community College; and GateWay Community College and the Maricopa Skill Center.

Up to this point, the school partners had had very few outside supporters, and as a result they felt overworked and undervalued. The community colleges' faculty, staff, and administrators listened to their concerns and studied their research and options. As a result of new relationships and information, programs were developed and tested among the PTT member colleges and schools, successes were celebrated, and members learned from failures. PTT adopted the philosophy of *failing forward* and considered ways to reward *interesting failures,* choosing to recognize the efforts of implementing teams rather than focusing only on successful outcomes. Community representatives became extended partners in an educational restructuring process and formed a Community Resources Group with a directory of more than a hundred contact listings for available services or materials for school needs. School personnel came to trust the community colleges as a credible convener. The state of the schools helped the colleges to build mutual trust, and MCCD helped address the schools' day-to-day problems by participating in program development and by providing office and staff support at all levels of organizational development. Figure 4.2 illustrates the major organizational levels of the Phoenix Think Tank.

Figure 4.2 Phoenix Think Tank Organization: 1994–1999

The challenges of creating this coalition included setting aside time to get to know one another, building trust among the various constituents, understanding one another's work, aligning individual priorities, keeping up with executive and key staff turnover, and reacting to outside school-reform pressures. Group members had to learn to think together in order to create a new institution from the best of their ideas. They were challenged to think outside of their "walls," to be proactive rather than reactive, and to suspend judgment long enough to understand what others were saying. A staff coordinator was essential for leading the team-building and program-design activities. As a contribution, MCCD provided a director to fulfill this role.

The primary difference between partnering and working as a coalition is that partners generally bring their individual experiences and resources to the community table for limited periods of time. The Cologne Project provides an example of partnering. With support from the Mott Foundation, eight PTT members traveled to Cologne, Germany, to learn about a project that allowed teachers to advance with their students from the first through the eighth grades. With further support from Mott, the project was replicated in the Roosevelt School District in south Phoenix. In this case, while coalition partners actively supported the idea through its implementation, they were not particularly involved in its design after it was turned over to the individual schools; instead, they were *partners* for the particular project. Sometimes a partnership, rather than a coalition, is all that is needed.

The Phoenix Think Tank is a *coalition:* Members interact with one another even when there is no special project, no funding sources, and no clearly identified action plan to pursue. The coalition members stay together because of a common mission: to help students. Members know each other, have a common vision, trust and respect each other. The personal nature of collaboration helps partners stay the course long enough to make an impact. Unlike partnerships, coalitions are self-sustaining, are driven by a broad, long-term goal, and support an ongoing process of improvement. They also form—and sustain—an extensive resource network and stand ready to receive projects, ideas, and funds quickly. They also are able to be competitive for grants since there is evidence of commitment and success. When leaders feel ownership of the collaborative process, they are generally quick to connect their work with other efforts to help create a large network of supportive groups. Figure 4.3 shows the Think Tank Collaborative Network.

Figure 4.3 Think Tank Collaborative Network

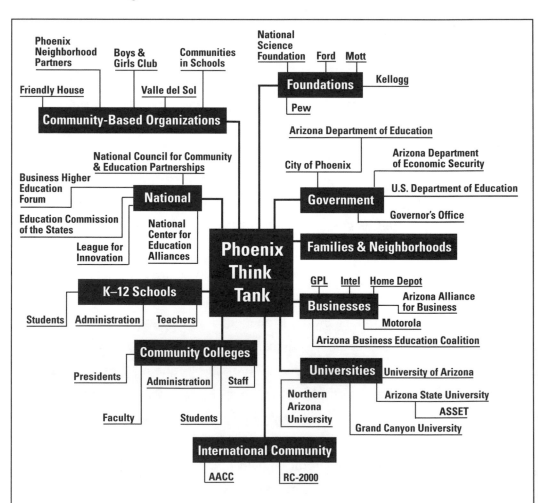

Moving from Thinking to Doing

The real developmental foundation for any group is the attitude of the players. Fostering an attitude of cooperation and dedication takes patience and skill, and the knowledge of how to engage individuals with varied backgrounds and priorities so that each feels valued and respected. This is a people process. In an organization such as the Phoenix Think Tank, individuals need to balance three forces: their volunteer commitment, their job expectations, and their personal values. A skilled community builder will guide the process and move aside to let leadership emerge from the group.

Some people are thinkers and others are doers. To serve the thinkers, at least 45 minutes of each PTT Steering Committee meeting was set aside for *open thinking,* during which attendees could describe their concerns, successes, and ideas. There was never enough time, but the open thinking period produced valuable learning and demonstrated respect for the coalition's partners, most of whom had become trusted friends. Session topics included the changing role of the teacher, all-day kindergarten, college requirements, school violence, workforce needs, and technology in the curriculum.

To satisfy the doers, members developed an action agenda of three systemic-change initiatives, which were based on the results of the best-practices study. Respondents in that study said that for learning conditions to increase student success, three things beyond academic training must be in place:

- Social services for students and their families
- Professional development opportunities for faculty, staff, and practitioners
- Positive outside-of-school growth experiences for students

Three Initiatives for Systemic Change

The 1994 Phoenix Think Tank two-day summer retreat was held in Prescott, Arizona. The 48 attendees included school superintendents and associate superintendents, college and university personnel, executives from community-building organizations and businesses, government representatives, and teachers. After exchanging many ideas and examples, attendees agreed on three large-scale systemic-change initiatives to meet school and community needs.

ExChange for Effective Learning (ExCEL) is a collaborative staff development process for K–16 faculty. This initiative integrates and coordinates staff and organizational development among K–12 school districts, high schools, MCCD institutions, Arizona State University, community-based organizations, and the business community. The staff development coordinators and directors come from PTT organizations. In one ExCEL project, the National Science Foundation provided funding to address science and mathematics competence. As a result of the project, math scores in Phoenix's inner-city elementary schools have surpassed statewide averages.

The Connectivity Project helps students achieve a seamless transition to the next level of learning, set goals, and see the relevance of their studies. The Achieving a College Education (ACE) program, for example, supports concurrent high school and community college enrollments and school-to-career activities that help students set realistic goals for their future. It also helps the large number of students who transfer from Maricopa's community colleges to Arizona State University.

This project meets PTT partners' common vision of connectivity: Students from kindergarten through graduate school are the accepted responsibility of all the partners, who believe "they are *all* our students." With the focus on the students, the group strives to see beyond petty differences and turf battles that could isolate members from one another and from the resources they need to improve learning environments.

Family Resource Centers provide counseling, health, and personal support services to students and their families at the school site. Family poverty, separation and loss, constant uprooting, and daily violence beleaguer many inner-city schools. The centers, staffed by trained human-services personnel, provide immediate, accessible relief for these problems, taking a tremendous burden off teachers' shoulders. They have quietly become trusted resources for parents, children, teachers, and community agencies.

After the Family Resource Center model worked in the Murphy Elementary School District under the leadership of Superintendent Bob Donofrio, nine other centers were established at inner-city elementary schools. Leaders for the project came from several sectors; Alex Pensiero, a creative retired Honeywell executive and the executive director of the Phoenix chapter of the Arizona Alliance for Business, was the earliest champion. His influence brought many new business supporters, and, working through the PTT coalition, Pensiero helped bring Communities in Schools (CIS) to Phoenix. CIS now provides many social services for students through the acquisition of community resources.

The Family Resource Centers also rely on organizations like the Boys and Girls Clubs and other community-based organizations, local churches, and state and local welfare and assistance agencies, including Arizona's Department of Economic Security.

Other PTT Projects

Technology resources can be a connecting force in education, but they are often distributed unequally among public schools, thus becoming something that divides people. For example, a school in the Nuestro Barrio section of Phoenix, one of Arizona's poorest areas, had one computer in the entire school in 1999. A year later, it was stolen. In a nearby suburban school in the Ahwatukee area, about six miles from

Nuestro Barrio, most students have their own computer and many have their own Web page.

MCCD insists that its colleges provide access to personal computers. At Glendale Community College, the two high-tech centers have more than 450 workstations, while the Mesa Community College information commons has more than 850. Each of the district's 10 colleges has computer access centers for all students.

Because MCCD and its Think Tank Department were positioned for opportunities in K–16 projects in fall 1999, MCCD received a federal Technology Innovation Challenge Grant to train approximately 3,000 K–12 teachers in unique and compelling uses of the Internet in class-rooms. This train-the-trainer project includes curriculum developed by the Stevens Institute of Technology, with support from the League for Innovation in the Community College.

Local schools' experience was invaluable to understanding what type of support was needed for this project. The teachers who are trained are linked through an e-mail list that lets them share problems, successes, and materials. The core trainers, provided by MCCD, provide training and extensive classroom follow-up with the teachers to guarantee that they implement newly learned skills and activities. This follow-up would not have been as effective without the prior relationships established through the PTT coalition.

At Phoenix College, a virtual learning community called Pueblo (1993–1999) helped K–8 students from Longview Elementary School travel, explore, and learn beyond their classrooms and their homes via the Internet. Longview students are generally poor and have limited use of the English language. Over 50 percent of them come from single-parent homes, and most have never left their neighborhood. Many are at risk of dropping out of school. Pueblo connected them to college-student and senior-citizen mentors who helped them think about themselves and their futures in new ways. Jim Walters, Pueblo's faculty director at Phoenix College, says, "What we're really doing is building a community that exists, not just in a virtual world, but in the real world, too."

A major benefit of the Pueblo experiment, teachers say, has been an improvement in student social skills, which helps introverted or troubled students to come out of their shells. Homeroom teacher Cyndy Olson relates, "One sixth grader who was withdrawn in the classroom became so engrossed with Pueblo that she began helping and teaching other students while she was online. Soon after, she was teaching her illiterate mother how to read using Pueblo. It helped her feel positive about herself and empowered her, and that carried over into the classroom."

The Pueblo project was created out of a discussion at a PTT meeting that focused on the potential value of computers in the classroom. The project received support from the Massachusetts Institute of Technology, Xerox Park, Apple Computer, and two U.S. Department of Education grants. Phoenix College committed personnel, facilities, and equipment to the project for several years. In addition to providing badly needed mentors for children who do not have strong support at home, the project connected students with experts around the world. It also allowed the college students who served as mentors to better understand the needs of younger students, and gave isolated homebound senior citizens a chance to be valued and even loved by their young admirers in Pueblo's online "K to Gray" subcommunity.

Technology can be a barrier to students who have neither the cultural advantages nor the wealth needed to participate in the new economies. Through the Pueblo project, MCCD has tried to remove that barrier.

Other K–16 Collaboratives Supported by Maricopa

The East Valley Think Tank

The East Valley Think Tank (EVTT) was formed in 1989 after Mesa Community College president Larry Christiansen approached colleagues in the East Valley of the Phoenix metropolitan area offering to help create a consortium to address issues facing educational leaders. He described the consortium this way:

> The EVTT is a consortium of educational institutions, representing kindergarden through university, banding together to deal with educational issues of common concern. Essentially, [it] will speak with one clear voice on the educational issues that impact the communities in the East (Phoenix) Valley. (Ronan 1994)

Christiansen believed that this educational consortium would be a driving force in the region's economic development efforts. The first meetings included the Mesa Public Schools, with representatives of MCCD's Phoenix Think Tank advising the process. The planning team suggested that all of the East Valley school districts, two additional community colleges (Chandler-Gilbert Community College and Scottsdale Community College), and Arizona State University be included in the consortium; the East Valley Partnership, a business group, also supported the EVTT. Mesa Community College provided the staff director, Bernie Ronan; a retired Mesa schools superintendent, Jim Zaharis, assisted with the coordination.

EVTT's first projects revolved around vocational education, dropout-prevention programs, foreign-language instruction, and teacher preparation. The foreign-language project was later disbanded and the dropout-prevention project became a multilateral partnership. Ronan comments on what might have improved the early stages of development:

> More time spent in sharing of ideas and concerns and
> brainstorming for the future would have been invaluable
> in the beginning years of the consortium. The East
> Valley Think Tank discovered that it needed to be about
> more than just 'cut and paste' replication of successful
> projects; it must also spend adequate time visioning a
> common future. (1994)

Ronan's admonition recalls the deliberative processes of the
Phoenix Think Tank. Allowing enough time for thinking and for sharing
ideas will contribute to any coalition's success.

The Phoenix Think Tank's earlier visioning did not include the
community college's role as a credible, neutral convener. That role
emerged very quickly for EVTT because of disputes over the reuse of a
large and valuable facility: The nearby Williams Air Force Base was on
the verge of closure. The base had been established in 1941, in what
was then a remote area in Mesa-Chandler, but as the area boomed after
World War II, housing and other development increasingly infringed on
the flight zone. When the 4,000-acre site and its three 10,000-foot runways
and 1.7 million square feet of buildings and facilities became available,
the governor issued a call for ideas for using the land and facilities.

Civic leaders, local mayors, and area residents saw the base closure
as a huge blow to the economic health of the community. Massive job
cuts and the loss of a significant payroll worried community leaders. The
motivation to recover these losses was extremely high and politically
charged. Competition among solutions and their proponents became
hotter, creating the potential for friction and bad feelings among the
leading contenders to reuse the base.

With a community-building and community-development mechanism
that already fixed upon school reform and cooperative educational
solutions, it was not long before EVTT was assigned the role of convener

and mediator for this community discussion. In August 1992, EVTT members participated in a visioning exercise to identify the positives and negatives of a collaborative use effort. Facilitators urged participants to identify their "best hopes" for partnerships in the reuse of the base and to think of the "worst fears" that could happen from collaborative planning and implementation. They also talked about the forces that favored and would deter successful cooperative use.

EVTT's monthly advisory board meetings often asked the public for reuse ideas. The plan that resulted called for the development of an education, research, and training (ERT) complex as a major component of the base redevelopment. The overall goal was to mix education, airport, and industrial uses and to replace the 4,000 lost jobs. Twenty-six educational institutions participated in ERT development—the largest collaboration around any base closure in the United States.

The next five years were not easy, but the resulting plan portioned the base's property assets among the partner institutions, and a new collaboration challenge was underway.

One project, spearheaded by MCCD governing board member and retired air force officer Donald Campbell, is Project Challenge, a highly successful boot camp for high school dropouts that operates through the Air National Guard on the base facilities. The Gila River Indian Community, whose ancestors farmed the land in prehistoric times, are partners in the airport operations and own rights to the former base golf course. An alternative high school operated by Maricopa County Schools gives students from East Valley school districts a second chance to graduate from high school. Workgroups use existing classrooms, housing, and meeting facilities for a collaborative training and staff development center whose offerings include aviation, high school programs, K–8 programs, medical training, and training for business and industry. The community colleges and the university offer credit courses. Former barracks and officer housing are now home to university and community college students.

West Valley Think Tank

The West Valley Think Tank, formed in 2000, is cochaired by Homero Lopez, president of Estrella Mountain Community College and a local school superintendent. The West Valley region includes Glendale Community College, the west campus of Arizona State University, school districts, and Goodyear Aerospace Company. The WVTT's activities center on legislation and policies that affect schools, with a special emphasis on student tests required by the Arizona Department of Education. The group focuses on improving the image of schools and communities in this formerly agricultural region of the valley.

Learning Connections

Learning Connections is a collaborative headquartered at Paradise Valley Community College since 1995, serving the north side of Phoenix. Despite rapid growth and numerous million-dollar homes, the Paradise Valley School District has a high percentage of children living in poverty and is plagued by high crime and gangs. Participants include the community college, Northern Arizona University, Arizona State University-West, and two unified school districts. Their well-organized committee structure addresses six goals:

1. Increase the number of highly qualified teacher candidates.
2. Develop strategies to identify and recruit a diverse student population.
3. Develop focused activities that inspire students to explore careers in teaching.
4. Provide support and guidance for students pursuing careers in teaching.
5. Develop and implement procedures to ensure ongoing communication and positive working relationships among partners.
6. Develop and implement procedures to measure outcomes, evaluate successes, and make modifications.

Members of Learning Connections believe that the residents, learners, and educational institutions of the North Valley will benefit from institutional cooperation. They chose not to use the term *think tank* in their name because it might convey a broader mission. Instead, they focus on specific tasks in a more structured approach to problem solving. Members also work toward continuous improvement of the institutional effectiveness of each member organization.

All of these collaboratives operate with a similar focus. Each has several large goals that address generic, macro-level issues, but their strategies and structures vary to meet the needs of individuals and communities. This practice means that the community owns the collaborative's vision and takes responsibility for achieving it. The leaders involved believe that facilitation and communication processes are critical to success. Without this support, these groups and their projects would not exist.

Murphy Elementary School District superintendent Bob Donofrio commented on the seamless system and broadly built partnerships, a consistent feature of macro-community development efforts:

> No longer can K–12 and higher education systems afford to work in isolation [from] each other. If we are going to produce students prepared for the 21st century workforce, we must create seamless systems by forging broad-based partnerships with each other and include community based organizations, government agencies, and the private sector as partners—not just as resources.

Chapter 5

Lessons and Recommendations

Synthesizing the complex lessons learned from community building is a challenge. The lessons listed here are primarily from the Maricopa Community College District's experience; they are offered to community colleges and others who seek to build community.

Lesson 1: People working on collaborative efforts need time to create a common vision.

As Ronan (1994) said, "The East Valley Think Tank discovered that it needed to be about more than just 'cut and paste' replication of successful projects; it must also spend adequate time visioning a common future."

> *Recommendation:* The members of a collaborative must develop and agree on both a vision for the future and a mission. Make time to think part of the agenda for every meeting, particularly at the formative stages of the collaborative. It is essential to develop a consensus on both a vision for a desired future and a mission showing the purpose of the collaborative.

Lesson 2: Partners should not be underestimated.

Elementary and secondary school personnel bring a broad range of skills and talents to the table, and their abilities should not be underestimated. In our work with MCCD's Phoenix Think Tank, we met teachers, principals, community organization staff, and school personnel who were dedicated and knowledgeable professionals.

> *Recommendation:* When working with the community, expect to be surprised by your community partners. Most will exceed your expectations and perform admirably if treated with respect and trust.

Lesson 3: A collaborative requires a mixture of programs and process to succeed.

Process and programs can change a system, connect people, and help students, and both are extremely valuable to the collaborative process. But it is easy to forget the value of good programs, and community-building participants can tire of process. Many need to see tangible results to maintain their interest. Achieving a balance between programs and process is not easy, but it helps a collaborative to succeed.

> *Recommendation:* Design agreed-upon strategies to appeal to different leadership styles and personal interests. Mix process and program at every opportunity. Select people to lead each area based on the ability to understand and convey the initiative's importance.

Lesson 4: People are encouraged by program success.

Program success stabilizes the community-building process. Roger Romero, superintendent of the Wilson Elementary School District in Phoenix, says, "What projects do is demonstrate in a small way what institutions should do in a big way." He adds, "As people can see what we are doing, they come to help. We need a good message, a clear vision, and proof that what we are doing is worthwhile."

> *Recommendation:* Use success stories to prove to participants that collaboration works. Tell these stories from the beneficiary's viewpoint or, when possible, invite the beneficiary to tell the story.

Lesson 5: Leaders will continue to question the collaborative's purpose if they do not feel that they have been consulted.

The Phoenix Think Tank was an experiment outside of state mandates and outside of the direction of the Maricopa Community College District's governing board. Even after the PTT established itself, gained national recognition, and became a model for foundations and educational associations, those not directly involved questioned what it was and why it existed. To prevent such questioning, coalition champions must clearly promote the collaborative's community-building strategy in ways that show value to a broad audience.

> *Recommendation:* Get full commitment from those at
> the top early in the community-building process. Provide
> feedback often, to help keep community-building efforts
> a priority with institutional CEOs.

Lesson 6: A collaborative needs to be constantly renewed.

A collaborative's need for a deep infrastructure of ownership and involvement never ceases. In the case of the Phoenix Think Tank, high turnover among school superintendents hindered the coalition throughout its history and made participation by deputy superintendents and middle managers critical to maintaining program continuity.

> *Recommendation:* Build provisions for sustainability so
> the collaborative's projects belong to the entire institution
> rather than to individual leaders. Continually introduce
> new leaders to projects, and conduct exit interviews with
> those who leave to determine possible reasons for
> dissatisfaction.

Lesson 7: A coalition thrives when its leaders share recognition with others.

Author and futurist Robert Theobald (1994) said, "You can either take the credit or have change." The more credit that Phoenix Think Tank members gave to others, the more credit returned to the coalition. The collaborative adopted the motto "The experts are among us." Participants were allowed the resources, confidence, and time to share with one another. Leaders became learners, and learners became leaders.

Recommendation: Pass credit and recognition around
the collaborative.

Lesson 8: People bond when they share a common language and understanding.

When collaborators move beyond their individual perspectives into the realm of common understanding, trust and friendship result. Building a common understanding took time for the Phoenix Think Tank coalition, and creating a common vocabulary made participants' voices clearer and more consistent. To facilitate understanding, one person was put in charge of vocabulary at each meeting to clarify language and acronyms not commonly understood; those who understood school reform helped those in the outside community understand it too.

Recommendation: Build a common language and provide
opportunities for interchange of terms and stories to
create a bond among participants.

Lesson 9: Others can use the coalition for worthy educational purposes.

The Maricopa Community College District had attempted to establish a mathematics and science improvement project at the elementary school, middle school, and high school levels. The National Science Foundation pumped more than $4 million into the project. The Phoenix Think Tank's image and network of existing school cooperation and support were valuable in building the project's credibility.

When the Stevens Institute of Technology was seeking demonstration sites for its AlliancePlus Project, MCCD was chosen as one of three sites because of the existing structure that connected colleges to schools in the PTT coalition. This five-year project to train teachers in the Phoenix area was developed with U.S. Department of Education funding. The far-reaching network allowed the project to expand to more than 2,000 teachers statewide by working with existing and new partners.

Recommendation: If the community-building collaborative is highly successful, carefully determine how it
might merge with or help with other large initiatives.
Think through the implications of such opportunities.
Use established premises to evaluate the reasons to take
on or not take on another partner or project.

Lesson 10: Technology helps bring people together.

The Internet can be a virtual "village well" where people build exciting
and viable communities. The Internet can also be used to strengthen
communication with remote populations. While e-mail and search
engines are not new, they can give us new insights on how to productively bridge local, national, and international communities.

Recommendation: Early in the collaborative's forma-
tive discussions, create a free-thinking technology unit
for community building. Use technology thoughtfully
and do not use it as a substitute for social space.

Lesson 11: Community projects are sometimes lost in the shuffle at the executive organizational levels.

The staff of an organization that assisted abused women shocked
the MCCD's executive cabinet with their descriptions of the realities of
battered women. The cabinet members were moved, but no program
ever materialized. Why?

First, a powerful board member brought the program to more than one
president, causing distrust and encouraging self-protection. If one president moved forward, it might have been perceived as upstaging another
president. The executive cabinet, which was positioned to act, froze.

Second, development takes time. College presidents are responsible
for the bottom line. They are charged with enrollment, revenue flow, and
return on investments. When do they have time to give to community
projects?

Without a mechanism ready to create a legitimate handoff of good project ideas, system responses can turn sluggish and awkward, and may result in lost opportunities to help students or communities. Furthermore, those who were disappointed may then broadcast that disappointment to opinion leaders and constituencies.

> *Recommendation:* In each community, empower one mechanism or person to provide intelligent coordination to community initiatives.

Lesson 12: Advance planning leads to successful program handoff.

How long should a community college's central office nurture a community-building program? When should it be handed off to another segment of the organization? How is budget transfer handled? How can you retain a financial seed if too much of the program's budget is handed off?

A collaborative must establish coordinating mechanisms that give its clients and customers an honest response. Collaborative planners should design appropriate links between the collaborative and community-based programs. At MCCD, the Office of the Community Agenda provided this mechanism for projects. A central office like that one can manage community-based organizations' proposals and advise a college or collaborative on proposal possibilities and available resources.

The first assumption of the Maricopa Office of the Community Agenda was that all programs were to be passed on to others. This was easier said than done, but as Table 5.1 illustrates, nearly all programs found a permanent home. Such handoffs show that programs also have greater chance of success when there is an established process for their thoughtful—and objective—review.

> *Recommendation:* Learn to estimate the likely duration of community programs. Assess the potential for program handoff and develop incentives for handing off programs successfully.

Table 5.1 Programs Transferred from Maricopa Office
of Community Agenda to Other Locations

Program	Current Location
Campus Compact (Service learning)	Mesa Community College houses the Campus Compact National Center for Community Colleges with programs housed at several of the district colleges.
Creative Pathways (Employee renewal through internship in the community)	The District's Human Resources and Employee Development Division now oversees this effort.
The Maricopa Institute for Arts, Entertainment, and Technology	Scottsdale Community College
Native American Program (Several facets from health issues to economic development)	Mesa Community College at Red Mountain
The Sedona Conferences and Conversations (An international gathering to converge education, entertainment, and technology innovations)	The private sector with national and international sponsorship
The Connectors Program (Linking citizens to social and human service referral on an everyday basis and at times of crisis)	Mesa Community College
Education Development Training Center (EDTC) (Create solutions for at-risk dropouts not associated with the educational system)	Mesa Community College; state and agencies
National Football League—Youth Education Team (A youth education center designed to introduce youth to technology)	South Mountain Community College and Rio Salado College

Lesson 13: Collaborative success must be measured both quantitatively and qualitatively.

However short-term and program-focused a collaborative might be, it must provide hard information for policymakers, funders, and participants. How many students were involved? How many business hours were contributed? How many people attended? Answering such questions usually requires quantitative measures, but facts and figures may not strengthen coalitions: Long-term commitment, values, vision, and tenacity may. Other factors come into play when evaluating a coalition's impact. How well did the partners communicate? Did the members address the real needs of the community? How did they know what those needs were? Assessment questions must also measure a team's long-term success.

> *Recommendation:* Design a process for evaluating the effectiveness
> of coalitions and community-building efforts, preferably early in the
> coalition's formation. Consider offering assessment training, including
> observation skills, to coalition managers and team leaders.

Lesson 14: Community colleges can play the role of convener with care and respect for potential partners.

Community colleges can act as conveners, calling the community together to discuss important issues. The members of MCCD's Phoenix Think Tank were surprised to learn that the community college was perceived as neutral in controversial political matters. The community colleges were also trusted and respected. Community colleges should reassess their influence and community credibility and be willing to be conveners, a natural and effective role for community colleges.

> *Recommendation:* Educate program and community leaders and
> college presidents, staff, and faculty about the convener's role and
> how it can be skillfully and effectively executed.

Chapter 6

Sustained Commitment Is the Key to Success

For community colleges, community building is difficult, not always rewarding, and hard to sustain even after tangible results have been achieved. It is also not often a criterion of career success for community colleges' chief executive officers, so CEOs who lead such efforts must be personally committed beyond their job descriptions.

CEOs and other education leaders often get drawn into a vortex of meetings, commissions, and councils that support the machinery of school and college operations. Most such activities have little to do with the real bottom line of school effectiveness—learning and student well-being—and they can occupy college personnel so completely that they have little time or energy left for community building. Superintendents, business executives, and college presidents often get up from a substantial dialogue to rush to another crisis meeting. It is not always easy to tell if these leaders are crisis driven or simply overscheduled. Making change in a community is difficult and requires a team effort. For lasting success, all community members must demonstrate an unwavering commitment to collaborate toward the common goal.

Collaboration seems to be an unnatural human act. Author and management consultant Peter Senge said, "In America, we shoot collaborators" (1994). The United States is a fast-paced, competitive nation. Collaboration takes time to learn and even more time to succeed. In a culture that rewards independent success at its highest levels, it is not surprising that community building is excluded from many community college goal statements.

The community college movement has grown at such a fast pace that we are only now seeing the long-term advantages of community building. Many community colleges do not yet have a solid, consistent identity as community builders. Although the respect for two-year colleges is increasing among political and business leadership, too few policymakers know that college personnel have the skills and experience needed to address a broad range of community problems. Legislative appropriations, board mandates, and faculty will rarely support community-building initiatives beyond education and training; however, we have experienced that dialogue will keep values clear and connected and will help to strengthen relationships, which, ultimately, may lead to the most valuable outcome of all—working together.

We are pleased that the entire Maricopa Community College District system adopted "community building" as its 2001–02 Honors Forum theme, that Mesa Community College added "building community" to its statement of shared values, and that MCCD governing board member Linda B. Rosenthal instituted a center for promoting civic participation. Such steps can only help MCCD's community-building image and increase its credibility. But the journey to making even deeper and more profound community changes will be long and challenging.

The following observations from partners in MCCD's community-building efforts represent the ideals of community building. They also express its difficulty and the distance community college leaders must still travel.

Rick Miller, past president of the Phoenix Metropolitan Boys and Girls Clubs and president and founder of a national nonprofit organization called Kids At Hope, Inc., points to the attitude adjustment needed for successful collaboration:

> Community-based organizations and education coalitions must learn to collaborate, but to do so, participants must suspend their self-interests and focus on the holistic success of all children.
>
> There have not been great strides in this direction. In medicine and business, for example, managers and leaders have learned breakthrough techniques to improve

their services. A large number of the community-based and education leadership is locked in old paradigms of self-interest. Suspending self-interest is a cultural change— a change that takes time and practice to learn.

Status quo thinkers have become accustomed to dealing with crises. They have not taken time to learn the difference between what is urgent and what is important. If we are to have effective community collaboration, we will need to look beyond self-interest and to the interests of children as a matter of the highest importance.

Luis Ibarra, executive director of Friendly House, a Phoenix Think Tank CBO, says, "The school doesn't represent the community, but it is a part of the community. Families need nontraditional thinking. We need to get beyond the politics, look at nontraditional initiatives together, and see what we can come up with."

Luz Sarmina Guiterrez, director of Valle del Sol Association to support successful Hispanic education and living, provides further perspective:

We are experienced service providers, and have valuable services to offer to students and their families. In spite of the schools' desire to include us in their programs, it is difficult for educators to understand the role the CBOs can play in the school setting. Once we can better understand each other, everybody will win. It takes lots of desire and collaboration, but the effort can lead to very good outcomes for all . . . the children and families . . . the schools and the CBOs.

School superintendent **Bob Donofrio** sums up the collaborative vision:

> I live and breathe collaboration every day to foster a coordinated system of care for our students. If we are to maximize learning outcomes for our students, we must concentrate on . . . what happens inside the schoolhouse as well as those social/environmental conditions that exist outside the schoolhouse. This is truly the only way we will help our students succeed. We must recognize that schools belong to the community and our allocation of resources and facilities must be commensurate with students and their family needs. We are all in this together, and sometimes we need to donate our resources to get more in return. In building community collaborations, we must develop a new attitude that makes us think about what resources we can bring to the table for the greater goodwill rather than what we can take away from the table.

The distinguished contributor to community development **John W. Gardner** argued that community is essential to ensure freedom itself and to allow humans to reach their potential:

> Without the continuity of the shared values that community provides, freedom cannot survive. Freedom is not a natural condition. Habeas corpus, trial by jury, a free press, and all the other practices that ensure our freedom are social constructions. . . . A community has the power to motivate its members to exceptional performance. It can set standards of expectation for the individual and provide the climate in which great things happen. It can pull extraordinary performance out of its members. The achievements of Greece in the 5th century B.C. were not the performances of isolated persons but of individuals acting in a golden moment of shared excellence. The community can tap levels of emotion and motivation that often remain dormant. . . . Humans need communities—and a sense of community. (1991, 5)

Board Policy for RC-2000 Community Colleges as Reported by Presidents

RC-2000 Survey Questions

March 2000   (22 responses)

Does your district/college have a board policy or goal that supports employee volunteer efforts during the business day?

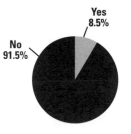

Does your district/college have a board policy or goal that restricts employees from providing community service during their workday?

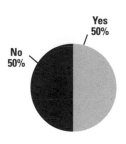

Does your district/college have staff or a budget designated for community development?

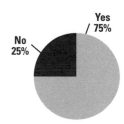

Does your district/college offer service learning programs for students?

Level of Support for Community Building from Board Members, CEOs, Staff, and Faculty

Board Members

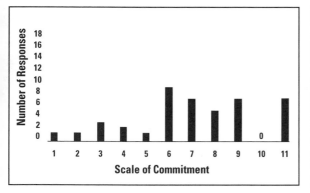

CEOs

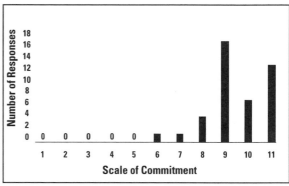

Staff Members

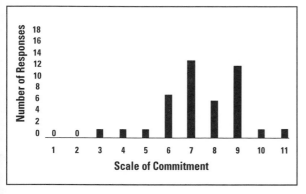

Faculty Members

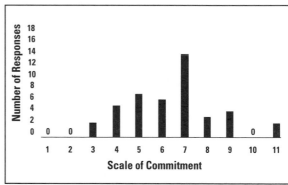

Source: AACC Presidents Academy, July 2000, Breckenridge, Colorado

Coalition Training Workshop Outline

Following is an outline of suggested topics for a series of interactive learning sessions designed to build greater understanding, mutual respect, and effective decision making among a diverse group of individuals.

Purpose

To assist partnership members in understanding the value of acting as a coalition; to help groups mature as quickly as possible for the good of each member and for the good of the communities they represent.

Outline

I. Determining the value of a partnership for you

Before any partnership can be functional, each partner must understand the commitment of time and other resources that will be necessary to achieve personal and professional goals. Members weigh the personal investment against the perceived value of the partnership.

II. Listing needs, limitations, and expectations

In a participatory process, members outline their need to collaborate as well as expected barriers and outcomes. This session also trains members to reassess the needs, barriers, and expectations annually.

III. Understanding priorities

Some priorities are stated openly; others are kept silent. Both types can strengthen or undermine the focus of a partnership. In a sharing, no-risk environment, partners learn how to unveil all priorities, build trust, and coordinate the group agenda with individual agendas.

IV. Achieving consensus

Most groups look for a compromise; the goal of this collaboration is to reach agreements that can be supported by each member of the team. This session shows how to reach consensus when partners disagree.

V. Writing the vision, mission, and goals statements

These road maps for the partners are complex to create when written in a spirit of total collaboration and consensus. To be valuable, the process needs to consider all viewpoints and to be facilitated in a way that enables everyone to support the statements.

VI. Defining a plan that is acceptable to all

Creating the plan is only one of the challenges for partnership members. Once they unveil a plan of action, there are others who need to "buy in." This session helps partners interact with this larger group to ensure that ownership and commitment are sufficient for implementation.

VII. Leading, managing, and following

Roles must be clear, must be accepted, and must meet the personal needs of partners and the overall need of the partnership to achieve its mission and vision. Participants analyze each role and determine who is best suited to fill it. Emphasis is placed on the idea that no role is more valuable than another; no person is more valuable than another.

VIII. Merging turfs for a bigger playing field

In an era of high need and low resources, education and business must find new resources and partners. This session uses an open dialogue to identify the needs, responsibilities, and opportunities for participants to allow others onto their turf.

IX. Going for the gold (finding additional resources)

Fundraising: Everyone wants it to happen; no one wants to do it. There are easy and fun ways to raise money and carry out the mission of the partnership at the same time.

X. Staying together

What happens when the partnership adds new clients or new programs? How do we keep good thinkers and workers energized and committed to the process? Does everyone understand the nature of systemic change and the time it takes to make a lasting impact? This session reveals the best practices for sustaining support.

XI. Defining the stages of partnership development

There are four stages of partnership development. With some clear examples and activities, members learn how to identify when their partnership is advancing and when it has stopped maturing or has regressed. Participants explore various ways to stimulate interest and commitment for greater satisfaction and productivity.

XII. Measuring impact and shortcomings

Documenting success is essential to continued support. Everyone wants to know how you are doing. This session uses examples of data collection and usage to stimulate discussion and planning.

XIII. Handling success and failure

Success may seem the easier of the two to handle, but failures do not have to be treated as disasters. In this session, partners learn how to recognize, analyze, strategize, and publicize both successes and failures to move the partnership forward.

XIV. Strategizing the next steps

A getaway retreat is an earned reward for their hard work. It is also a valuable way to gain the members' uninterrupted attention while they plan for the next year's work and beyond. How much work is involved? How much will it cost? Will people come? What does a program look like? All of these questions—and more—are discussed in this session.

XV. Expanding the membership

The right mix, the right talents, the right attitude, the right resources—all determine if a partnership will be productive or a waste of valuable time. This session helps people find their best avenues for growth.

XVI. Celebrating the successes—together!

Celebrations should occur throughout the planning, implementation, and evaluation stages. Different personalities wish to celebrate in different ways. This session reviews the options and includes discussion of how celebrations can complete a process while beginning a new phase.

Visioning and Values Workshop: Key Values

_____ ACHIEVEMENT

To accomplish something important in life, be involved in significant activities, succeed at what I am doing.

_____ AESTHETICS

To be able to appreciate and enjoy beauty for beauty's sake, to be artistically creative.

_____ AUTHORITY / POWER

To be a key decision maker directing priorities, the activities of other people, and/or allocation and use of general resources.

_____ ADVENTURE

To experience variety and excitement, and to be able to respond to challenging opportunities.

_____ AUTONOMY

To be independent, have freedom, be able to live where I want to live and do what I want to do.

_____ HEALTH

To be physically, mentally, and emotionally well, to feel energetic and maintain a sense of well-being.

_____ INTEGRITY

To be honest and straightforward, just and fair.

_____ INTIMACY / FRIENDSHIP / LOVE

To have close personal relationships, experience affection, share life with family and friends.

_____ PLEASURE

To experience enjoyment and personal satisfaction from the activities that I appreciate.

_____ RECOGNITION

To be seen as successful, receive acknowledgment for achievements.

_____ SECURITY

To feel stable and comfortable with few changes or anxieties in my life.

_____ SERVICE

To contribute to the quality of life for other people and to be involved in improving society or the world.

_____ SPIRITUAL GROWTH

To have communication or harmony with the infinite source of life.

_____ WEALTH

To acquire an abundance of money and/or material possessions; to be financially independent.

_____ WISDOM

To have insight, be able to pursue new knowledge, have clear judgment, and be able to use common sense in life situations.

Assume your situation is such that you HAVE to give up 10 of these values. Which would they be? Drop them out by putting an X in the left column. Now rank the order for your top five value preferences, from highest (1) to lowest (5).

Source: Rouse 1986

References

Allen, Michael. 1998. "Welfare Reform: Creating Opportunities or Increasing Obstacles?" Denver: Education Commission of the States. 1998.

Commission on the Future of Community Colleges. 1988. *Building Communities: A Vision for a New Century*. Washington, D.C.: American Association of Community and Junior Colleges.

Day, Mary. 1999. "Report on the Board Ends." Internal report to the Maricopa Community College District governing board. March, Tempe, Ariz.

Gardner, John W. 1991. "Building Community." *Independent Sector* (September): 5.

Gleazer, Edmund J., Jr. 1995. Introduction to *The Company We Keep: Collaboration in the Community College*, by John E. Roueche, Lynn Sullivan Taber, and Suanne D. Roueche. Washington, D.C.: Community College Press, American Association of Community Colleges.

———. [1980] 1998. *Community Colleges: Values, Vision, and Vitality*. Reprint, with foreword by Dale F. Campbell. Washington, D.C.: Community College Press, American Association of Community Colleges.

Harlacher, Ervin L., and James F. Gollattcheck. 1996. *The Community-Building College: Leading the Way to Community Revitalization*. Washington, D.C.: Community College Press, American Association of Community Colleges.

Jacobson, David. 2001. "Stakeholder Learning Collaborative Pilot Project." Unpublished proposal/prospectus. New York: Wagner Graduate School of Public Service, New York University.

Jarman, M. 1999. "Phoenix Area Jobs to Double in 25 Years." *The Arizona Republic*, 30 March.

Maricopa Community College District (MCCD). 1999. *Maricopa Community College District Policy Manual*. Phoenix: Maricopa Community College District.

Ronan, Bernie. 1994. "Collaboration in Action: The East Valley Think Tank and the Reuse of Williams Air Force Base." Published for internal use by Mesa Community College, Center for Public Policy and Service, Mesa, Ariz.

Rouse, Ken. 1986. *Putting Money in Its Place*. Boston: New England Financial Advisors.

Senge, Peter. 1994. Comments before the Sloan Institute on Learning Organization and Change, Massachusetts Institute of Technology, Boston.

Theobald, Robert. 1994. Comments at Phoenix Think Tank All-Teams Meeting, Phoenix Metropolitan Boys and Girls Clubs, January.

Index

About the Authors

Paul A. Elsner is chancellor emeritus of the Maricopa Community College District, where he helped develop many college community initiatives during his 22-year tenure. He completed his doctorate at Stanford University and was a Kellogg Fellow there. Elsner is a graduate of Harvard's Institute for Educational Management. He holds a master's and bachelor's degree in English and has taught English at the university, college, and high school levels. Among the many coalitions and community network associations Paul has founded are the Phoenix Think Tank, an urban-based K–16+ community coalition; and RC-2000, a federation of the largest urban community college districts in the United States, Canada, and Great Britain. Elsner worked for 10 years with Janet Beauchamp Clift in her roles as the executive director of both the Phoenix Think Tank and RC-2000. Elsner founded and continues to lead the Sedona Conferences and Conversations, a forum that looks at the international social implications of technology. He has written numerous articles on topics ranging from civic participation to leadership development. He is a frequent national and international speaker and consultant.

Janet Beauchamp Clift gained perspective on community building from more than 25 years of work in K–12 schools, large and small businesses, nonprofit associations, universities, and community colleges. In her role as director of the Think Tank Department at Maricopa Community College District since 1992, she manages collaboration projects to strengthen relationships and leadership opportunities among business, education, and community representatives. The efforts involve local, national, and international partners. National partners include the Ford, Kellogg, Pew Trusts, and Mott Foundations and the U.S. Department of Education, Bank Street College, Stevens Institute of Technology, American Association of Community Colleges, and the League for Innovation in the Community College.